WRITE IT DOWN

An ESL Composition Text

WRITE IT DOWN

An ESL Composition Text

Jeanne Portnoy James

Holt, Rinehart and Winston
New York Chicago San Francisco Philadelphia Montreal Toronto
London Sydney Tokyo Mexico City Rio de Janerio Madrid

Library of Congress Cataloging-in-Publication Data
James, Jeanne Portnoy.
Write it down.

1. English language—Text-books for foreign speakers. 2. English language—Rhetoric. I. Title.
PE1128.J32 1986 808′.042 86-19505

ISBN 0-03-000174-9

Address correspondence to:
383 Madison Avenue
New York, N.Y. 10017

Printed in the United States of America
Published simultaneously in Canada
7 8 9 0 090 9 8 7 6 5 4 3 2 1

Holt, Rinehart and Winston
The Dryden Press
Saunders College Publishing

Preface

Write It Down, which is written for the beginning to low-intermediate ESL student, developed out of my several years of teaching composition in an intensive English program.

Write It Down teaches students the complete writing process, giving low-level ESL students the skills needed to develop surprisingly sophisticated compositions. Students are able to make considerable progress with their writing. Generating ideas, organizing ideas, focusing, revising and proofreading are emphasized. Exercises take the students through each step, helping them learn how to write.

The organization of the textbook is cyclical in nature. The writing process is reintroduced in each lesson, while emphasizing a different step each time. Common methods of organization (narration, description, process, and comparison/contrast) are taught within the framework of the process.

Connectors and transition words are also covered. Each lesson also includes proofreading exercises that focus on errors commonly made by students at this level. Some of these include agreement, verb tense, run-ons, and fragments.

As mentioned above, this book is written for the beginning to low-intermediate ESL student. It assumes that the student can write, in legible handwriting, a short, controlled composition using short, simple sentences. All of the sample compositions presented in this text were written by students at this level.

The philosophy of this text is that writing is a learnable and exciting process of creation. By developing this process, students can see their thoughts, feelings, and ideas come alive on paper. For students who are just beginning to communicate effectively in English, this is an encouraging experience. They will have developed important "how to" skills—how to generate ideas, get them down on paper and organize them. Skills such as grammar, spelling and vocabulary will improve with time and enhance their writing ability. The main emphasis of *Write It Down* is to develop a strong foundation that can be built on as the student learns more English.

This book could not have been written without the help and encouragement of a great many people. I must first thank all my colleagues at the Spring International School including Pambos Polycarpou, the school director, and all the teachers who used these pages in their classes. Special thanks go in particular to Connie Shoemaker, whose enthusiasm and support kept me going. For their helpful suggestions, I would like to thank the following reviewers: Debra Deane Matthews, University of Akron; Cherie Lenz-Hackett, University of Washington; Bruce Southard, Oklahoma State University; Jean Zukowski/Faust, Northern Arizona University; Sherry Southard, Oklahoma State University; Lynette Black, Memphis State University; Amy Sonka, Boston University. My final thanks go to my husband, Ken James, for his patience and understanding, and to my parents who have encouraged my writing since my childhood.

Jeanne Portnoy James

Contents

Lesson Seven Process 79

Lesson Eight Comparison and Contrast 93

Lesson Nine Using Reasons and Examples for Support 109

Appendix 127

Lesson One
Basic Mechanics

Introduction

What is a paragraph? A paragraph is a group of sentences that are about the *same* idea or topic. Sometimes a paragraph is a complete unit. Sometimes it is part of a much longer piece of writing.

Read these two groups of sentences. Which one is a paragraph?

1. My name is George Ríos. I am from Bogotá, Colombia. I came to the United States to study English. I want to be a businessman. I need to learn English to be a good businessman.

2. My name is George Ríos. Bogotá is the capital of Colombia. English is an important language for business. Good businessmen need to speak English.

What is 1 about? What is 2 about? Which is a better paragraph, 1 or 2? Why?

____

____

____

FOCUS Punctuation Marks and Their Names

.	period	This sentence ends with a period.
,	comma	I need books, pens, and paper.
:	colon	I bought these items: books, pens, and paper.
;	semicolon	These two sentences are closely related; connect them with a semicolon.
?	question mark	Is this a question mark?
’	apostrophe	He doesn’t speak Spanish.
“ ”	quotation marks	“Those are my exact words,” he said.
!	exclamation point	What a nice surprise!
-	hyphen	Use a hyphen when a long word comes at the end of a line and it is neces- sary to divide the word.

FOCUS Rules for Composition Titles

1. Always begin the first word of a title with a capital letter.
2. Always begin the last word of a title with a capital letter.
3. Begin all other words of the title with a capital letter except for
   articles (a, an, the)
   short prepositions (in, on, at, to, of, by, for, with)
   the word *and*
4. Center the title at the top of the page.

Exercise A: The following are titles of famous books and stories. Rewrite them, using capital letters where they are necessary.

1. war and peace ______________________________
2. a tale of two cities ______________________________
3. the merchant of venice ______________________________
4. the old man and the sea ______________________________
5. an egyptian childhood ______________________________

6. murder on the orient express ______

7. romeo and juliet ______

8. death of a salesman ______

9. of time and the river ______

10. travels with charlie ______

FOCUS How Your Composition Should Look

1. The title is at the top of the page and in the center.
2. Indent each new paragraph.
3. The left margin should be straight.
4. The right margin will not be straight, but it should be neat.

1 Title

2 XXX XXXXX XXXX XXXXX XXXXXXXXX. XXXXX XXXX XXXXX XXX XXXXX. XXXXXXX XXXXX XXXXX XXXX XXXX XX XXXXX. XXXX X XXXX XXX XXX XXXXXXX XXXX XXX.

2 XXXX XXXXX XX XXXXX XX XXXXXXX. XXXX XXXX XXXX XXX XXXXX XXXX XXX XX X. XXXXX XXXXX XXXX XX XX XX XXXX.

2 XXXXX XXXX XXX XX X XX XXX XX. XXXX XX XXX XXXX XXXX. XXXXXXXX XXXXXX XXXXX XXXX XX XXXXX XXXX.

3 Left margin — 4 Right margin

FOCUS Basic Capitalization and Punctuation Rules

1. Begin every sentence with a capital letter.
2. Put a period at the end of every sentence unless it is a question or an exclamation.

3. Write all names with capital letters. This includes names of
   people (John, Mohamed)
   places (New York, Central Park)
   schools, companies, buildings (Rice University, Sultan Oil Company, the Empire State Building)
   days of the week (Sunday, Monday, . . . Saturday)
   months (January, February, . . . December)
   languages and nationalities (Chinese, Arabic)
   the names of famous places and landmarks (the Eiffel Tower, the Pyramids, the Statue of Liberty)
4. Always write the word *I* with a capital letter.
5. Put a comma between a city and a country or a city and a state. (Tokyo, Japan) (Houston, Texas)
6. Put a comma between the date and the year. (July 17, 1953)
7. Put a comma between the day and the month. (Tuesday, March 2)

Exercise B: Capitalization Correct these sentences by changing lower-case letters to capital letters where it is necessary.

1. josé is a student at denver university.
2. he doesn't speak english very well.
3. he is my friend.
4. i help him with his english.
5. he helps me with my spanish.
6. josé will go to new york on monday.
7. his flight to new york is at 7:00.
8. i will drive him to stapleton international airport in my toyota.
9. he will come back to denver on june 16.
10. i will take him to a very nice french restaurant when he returns.

Exercise C: Punctuation Add commas and a period to each sentence as necessary.

1. I was born in Queens New York on July 17 1953

2. In September 1980 I moved to San Francisco California

3. Now I am living in Osaka Japan

4. Next year I will move to Riyadh Saudi Arabia

5. I will live in Saudi Arabia until March 11 1989

Exercise D: Correct the mistakes in capitalization and punctuation in each paragraph.

Today is saturday march 12 1985 I am sitting at my desk i am writing a letter to my friend joe tomorrow is joe's birthday he will be 28 years old I am sad because i can't go to his birthday party

Anne is a french student at the spring international school in denver colorado she is studying english and business anne wants to be a manager of a company when she returns to france

next month i am taking a trip to italy with a friend we will be there for three weeks we leave on wednesday april 18, and return on wednesday may 8 i don't speak italian well, but i am sure we will have a good time

FOCUS Proofreading Symbols

When your teacher corrects your composition, he or she may put some *symbols* (special marks) on your paper. These symbols will show you where you made mistakes. They will also show you what kind of mistakes you have made. Your job is to correct the mistakes.

You will learn some symbols in this book. In this lesson, you will learn three symbols: **cap**, **p**, and **sp**.

1. *cap* You need a capital letter.

   Example: John lives in california. (cap)

2. *p* You have a mistake in punctuation. Add or change the punctuation.

   Example: I bought apples (p) oranges (p) and bananas (p)

3. *sp* You have made a spelling mistake.

   Example: John is studing (sp) English.

Let's practice these three symbols.

Exercise E: Use the symbols to correct the mistakes in each paragraph. Then rewrite each paragraph.

Nancy lives in Cairo (p) egypt (cap) She is studing (sp) arabic (cap) at the university. She likes cairo (cap) very much.

____

____

____

Nancy lives on mohamed hagagul street it is a busy street near the university it is very nosy.

Exercise F: Find the 15 mistakes in this paragraph. Then rewrite the paragraph.

Aziza is from rabat morocco. she is studing english in the united states She lives in portland, oregon with an american family. aziza is very happy living in america.

Sentence Boundaries

Look again at the second paragraph that you corrected in Exercise E (p. 6). This paragraph consists of three sentences:

Nancy lives on Mohamed Hagagul Street.
It is a busy street near the university.
It is very noisy.

How do you know when to begin a new sentence? Every simple English sentence has a subject and a verb.

Examples: John works.
Mary is sleeping.

Most sentences also have a complement. The complement comes after the verb. It makes the sentence more interesting by adding more information.

Examples: John works hard every day.
Mary gave Tom a birthday present.

A simple sentence can have a compound subject. (This means that it has two subjects before the verb.)

Example: Phil and Martha have two children.

A simple sentence can also have a compound verb.

Example: Phil and Martha live and work in Boston.

A simple sentence cannot have a new subject after the verb. If you put a new subject after the verb, you must begin a new sentence. Put a period at the end of the first sentence. Begin the new sentence with a capital letter. You cannot put a comma between the two sentences. You must use a period and a capital letter.

Incorrect: Phil is a teacher, he teaches in a high school.
Correct: Phil is a teacher. He teaches in a high school.

Exercise G: For each item, write next to the number of the sentence **C** for correct or **I** for incorrect. Then correct the mistakes.

1. Phil began teaching ten years ago. He really enjoys his job.

2. Phil teaches history and geography, he also coaches football after school.

3. Phil's wife, Martha, is a lawyer in a small law firm.

4. Martha thinks her job is very interesting, she meets a lot of different people in her work.

5. Phil and Martha work very hard, they don't often go out during the week.

6. They enjoy their weekends together very much. They like playing tennis and going to movies.

Exercise H: Correct this paragraph. There are four mistakes.

Paul decided that he wanted to take a vacation. He went to a travel agent for some information, the travel agent suggested several places. Paul thought about it for a while, he decided to go to Mexico for a week and relax on the beach.

Writing Assignment

Interview a classmate about one of these topics: his or her job, family, or career plans. Write one paragraph about what you learn.

Exchange papers with your classmate when you finish. Check the punctuation and spelling. Your teacher will help you.

Lesson Two
The Writing Process

Introduction

Writing a good composition is not easy. You must follow many steps.

Writing is similar to building a house. If you build a house, you must follow many steps. What are these steps?

1. *Get some ideas*. Do you want a big house or a small house? How many rooms? How many floors? What materials will you use?

2. *Organize your ideas.* Put your ideas together. Where do you want the kitchen? Where do you want the living room?

3. *Write a plan.* Write down your ideas. You can study them and check them.

4. *Make changes.* After you study your ideas, you may need to make some changes. Perhaps you will decide that you want another bedroom. Or maybe you will decide to put a fireplace in the living room.

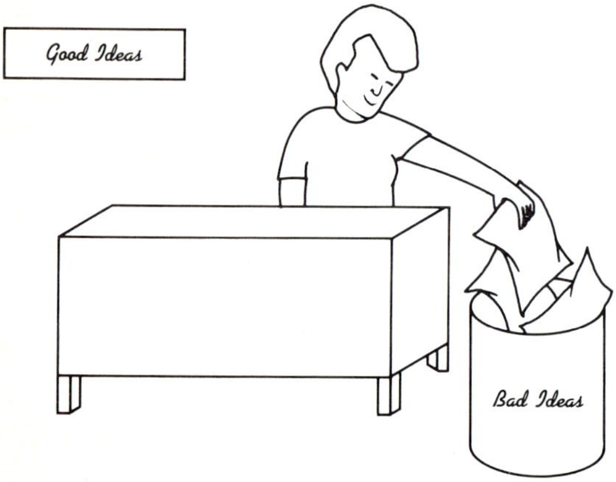

5. *Make your final plan.* Put all your ideas together.

6. *Check everything carefully.* Make sure that you don't have any mistakes. Make sure that you didn't forget anything important.

When you write a composition, you need to follow many steps, too. You cannot build a house without making a plan. You cannot write a good composition without making a plan.

These are the steps to follow when you write a composition. You will see that they are very similar to the steps for building a house.

FOCUS The Writing Process

Step 1: Generate Ideas
Generate means "make" or "create." In this step, you decide what you want to write about. You get your ideas and write them down.

Step 2: Organize Your Ideas
In this step, you put your ideas together. You decide which ideas work well together. You decide which ideas are useful.

Step 3: Write Your First Draft
The first draft is the first copy of your composition. It is not the final copy. You will change this copy several times before you are finished.

Step 4: Revise
Revise means "change." Here, you make changes in your composition.

Step 5: Rewrite
After you make your revisions (changes), write your composition again.

Step 6: Proofread
Read your work. Check your grammar, spelling, and punctuation. Correct your mistakes.

Step 7: Choose a Title
Remember that every composition must have a title.

This textbook will help you learn how to write a good composition. You will learn how to do each of the seven steps.

Let's begin!

FOCUS General Topics and Specific Examples

What is a general topic?

What is a specific example?

Look at the general ideas and specific examples on the next page.

1. *General topic:* subjects at school
   Examples: mathematics
   English
   chemistry
   physics

2. *General topic:* clothing
   Examples: shoes
   hat
   pants
   sweater

You can also go from general to specific in steps.

1. *General topic:* clothing
   Example: women's clothing
   More specific examples: skirt, dress, blouse

2. *General topic:* subjects at school
   Example: science
   More specific examples: physics, biology, chemistry

You can use a tree diagram to show your ideas.

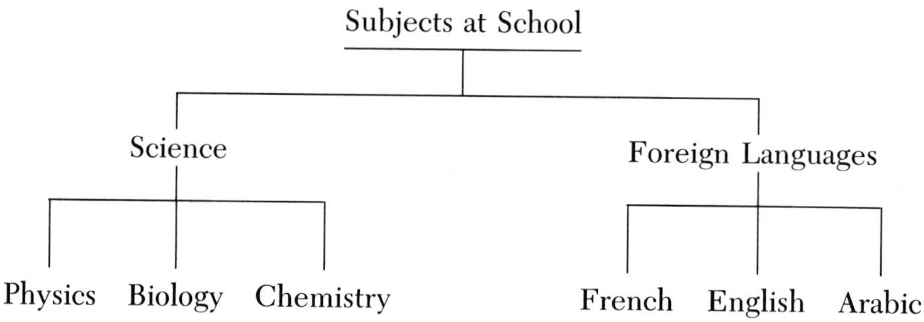

You can also use a circle diagram to show general and specific ideas.

Clothing
Women's clothing

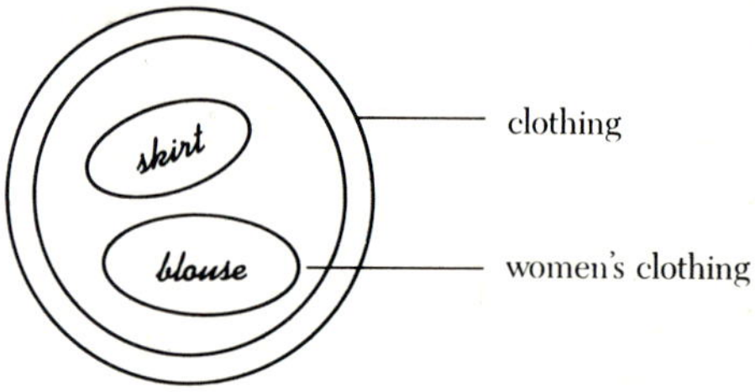

Exercise A: Complete this diagram.

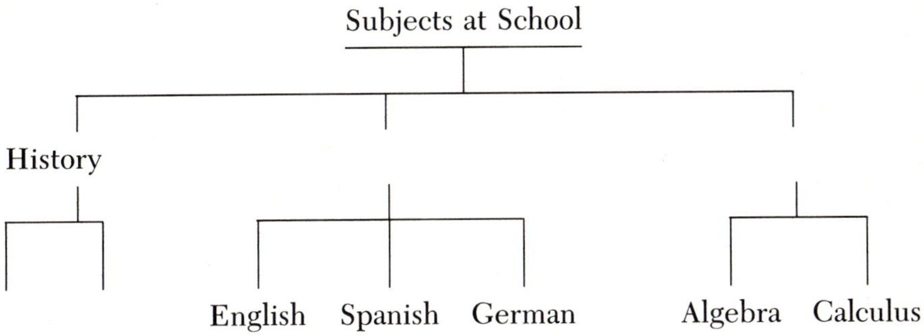

Exercise B: Order each group of words from general to more specific.

1. Water sports/sports/swimming/fishing

   General topic: ______________________________

   Example: ______________________________

   More specific examples: ______________________________

2. Pen/writing tool/pencil/tools

   General topic: ______________________________

   Example: ______________________________

   More specific examples: ______________________________

Exercise C: Work with a classmate. For each general topic, write your own examples and more specific examples. When you finish, compare your answers with those of other students.

1. General topic: food

   Example: ______________________________

   More specific examples: ______________________________

2. General topic: weather

   Example: ______________________________

   More specific examples: ______________________________

3. General topic: animals

   Example: ______________________________

   More specific examples: ______________________________

4. General topic: beverages

   Example: ______________________________

   More specific examples: ______________________________

5. General topic: magazines

   Example: ______________________________

   More specific examples: ______________________________

6. General topic: countries

   Example: ______________________________

   More specific examples: ______________________________

FOCUS Using the Writing Process

Step 1: Generating Ideas

Let's say you want to write a composition about the weather. *Weather* is your general topic. You will need some examples and specific ideas about the weather. Write down all the words you think of when you think about the weather.

hot *in my country* *snow*
cold *in the United States* *fog*
rain *dry*
sun *humid* *wind*

Step 2: Organizing Ideas
Put your ideas together. Decide which ideas are general. Decide which ideas are specific. Decide which ideas go together.

weather

in my country *in the United States*

hot *humid* *rain* *wet* *hot* *dry* *sun* *dusty*

Look carefully at the list of ideas. Then look carefully at the diagram. Are all of the ideas in the list also in the diagram?

> You do not have to use all the ideas in your list. Choose the ideas that you want to use.

Look at the diagram again. Are all of the ideas in the diagram from the list? What about *wet* and *dusty*?

> Sometimes you will think of more ideas after you finish your list. Add them to your diagram. They may be very good ideas!

Step 3: Writing the First Draft
Now you can begin writing. Remember that this is only the first draft. You will make many changes.

In my country, the weather is always hot. It is usually humid. It rains a lot. Everything is wet. In the United States, it is hot. It is dry. There is a lot of sun. It is very dusty.

Step 4: Revising

In this step, you make changes. Ask yourself these questions.

1. Does the composition have enough information?
2. Do you have some questions that the composition doesn't answer?
3. Is the information in the composition correct?

Here are some examples of how to use the questions above.

1. Does the composition have enough information?
   What is the student's country?
   Which part of the United States is the student writing about? The United States is very big. Different parts have different kinds of weather.
2. Do you have some questions that the composition doesn't answer?
   What season is the student writing about? The weather is not the same in every season.
3. Is the information in the composition correct?
   Is the weather in the United States always hot?
   Again, what season is the student writing about?

You can ask yourself one more question.

4. This paragraph is about weather. Specifically, the writer is comparing the weather in his or her country with the weather in the United States. This composition has only one paragraph. Remember that in a paragraph, all the sentences should be about the same idea.

   How many paragraphs does the writer need?

Step 5: Rewriting

In this step, you use the changes that you made to write the composition again. Here is the new composition. You can see the changes.

I am from Thailand. In my country, the weather is always hot. It rains a lot. It is usually humid. Everything is wet.

Now I am living in New Mexico, in the United States. In the summer, New Mexico is very hot and dry. There is a lot of sun. It is very dusty.

Does this draft:

have enough information?
answer your questions?
have correct information?
have a new paragraph for each new idea?

FOCUS Proofreading Symbols

In Lesson One, you learned three proofreading symbols. They were:

cap You need a capital letter.
p You have a punctuation mistake.
sp You have a spelling mistake.

Here is one more symbol: ¶.

¶ You need a new paragraph because you have a change in ideas. Indent.

Exercise D: Here is the first paragraph of the composition. It has some mistakes. Use the symbols to correct the mistakes. Then rewrite the paragraph.

cap *cap* *sp* *cap* *sp*
¶ I am from thailand. in my contry, the weather is always hot it is usualy
p
cap
humid. It rains a lot. everything is wet
p

____

____

____

Exercise E: Here is the second paragraph of the composition. It has 11 mistakes. Find the mistakes. Then rewrite the paragraph.

now I am living in new mexico It is in the united states. in the summer, New Mexico is very hot and dry. there is a lot of sun it is very dusty

____

____

____

Step 6: Choosing a Title

You can choose a title for the composition before you write it or after you have finished it. Usually it is easier to choose the title after you have finished the composition.

Remember to put the title at the top of the page, in the center. Follow the rules for capitalization of titles on page 2.

Exercise F: Here are some possible titles for this composition. Rewrite them, using correct capitalization.

1. the weather in two places ______________________________
2. different weather ______________________________
3. a change of weather ______________________________

Writing Assignment

Go back to Exercise C on page 15. You and your classmates will choose one of the topics in this exercise to practice the writing process that you learned in this lesson. Work with your classmates and teacher to generate and organize your ideas. Then write your composition. Don't forget to revise and proofread.

Lesson Three
Describing an Object

Introduction

Imagine that a friend in your English class does not understand the word *apple*. If you speak the same language, you can translate the word *apple*. You can tell your friend the word for apple in your native language.

But what if you and your friend do not speak the same language? Maybe you will say in English, "An apple is a fruit. It is round and hard. Most apples are red, but some are yellow or green." You will *describe* an apple.

Here is some special vocabulary that we use to describe things.

***1. Color*:** **red / blue / yellow / green / orange / brown / purple / gray / pink / black / white** There are many other colors, but these are the most common.

Exercise A: Sometimes colors have different meanings to people from different cultures. Answer the following questions. Write the color in the space. Then compare your answers with those of your classmates.

1. Which color is a happy color? ______________________

2. Which color is an angry color? ______________________________

3. Which color is a sad color? ______________________________

4. Which color reminds you of death? ______________________________

5. Which color is for kings, queens, or other important people?

____

6. What is your favorite color? ______________________________

2. *Size:* enormous / large / small / tiny / tall / short / wide / narrow / long

Exercise B: Fill in each space with an appropriate adjective from the list above.

Costa Rica is a beautiful country in Central America. San José is its capital. San José is a __________ city with a population of approximately one million. The main streets of San José are __________ and __________.

Santa Marina is a very __________ village in the mountains. Its population is only 350. The streets of this village are __________ and winding.

Costa Rica is famous for its coffee and bananas. The banana trees are very __________. They grow on __________ banana plantations in the jungle.

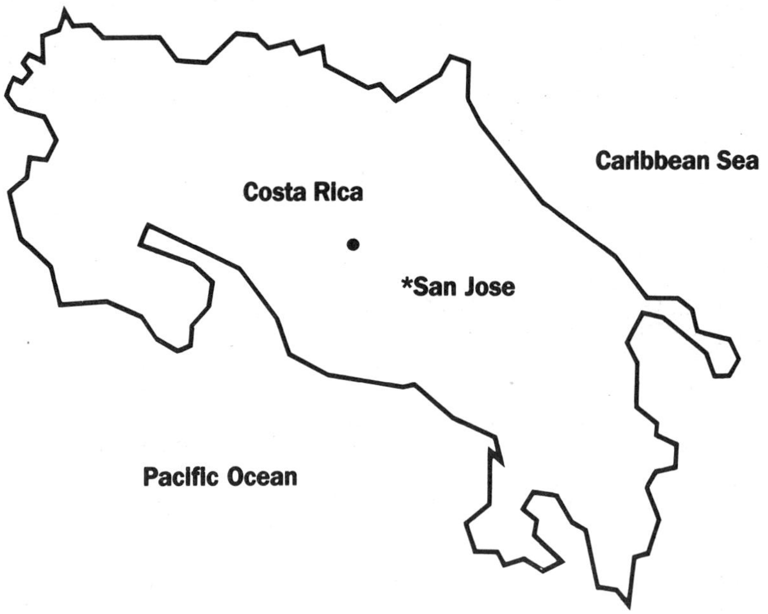

3. *Shape:*

Shape:

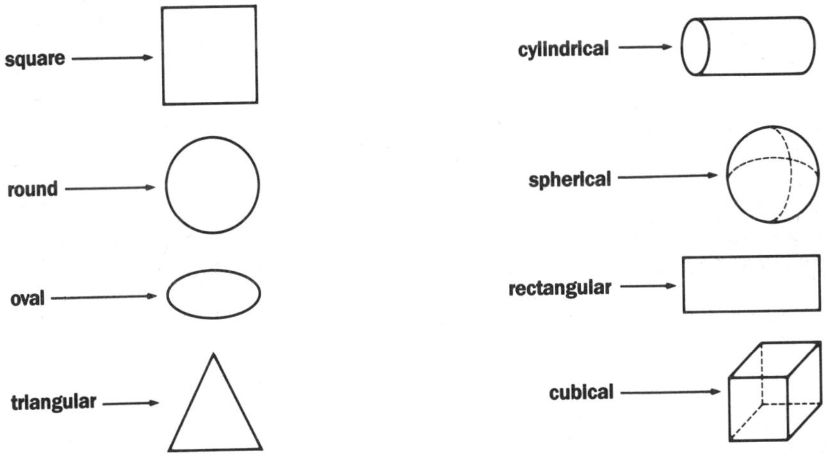

Exercise C: Follow the example. Complete each sentence with a word that describes the shape of the object. Compare your answers with a classmate's.

Example: This piece of paper is ___rectangular___.

1. An apple is ________________.
2. Eggs are ________________.
3. A soccer ball is ________________.
4. A baseball bat is ________________.
5. Oranges are ________________.
6. My notebook is ________________.

4. Material: **wood / plastic / paper / metal / glass / clay** When we talk about material, we use the phrases *made of* or *made out of.*

Exercise D: Follow the example. Complete each sentence with one or more words that tell what the object is made of. Compare your answers with a classmate's.

Example: This chair is made of ___wood___.

1. A bottle is made of ________________.
2. Ballpoint pens are made of ________________.
3. Windows are made out of ________________.
4. My pencil is made of ________________.
5. A pair of scissors is made of ________________.
6. A kite is made out of ________________.
7. Most flower pots are made of ____________, but some are made of ____________.

FOCUS: Choosing a General Topic and Focusing

Suppose you want to describe an object that is common in your country, but is not common in other countries. Your *general topic* is an object which is common in your country.

How do you begin?

First, you decide which object you want to describe. Here are some ideas that can help you choose the object.

1. Choose an object that you know very well.
2. Choose an object that is easy for you to describe. For this exercise, do not choose an object that has many parts.
3. Choose an object that is interesting.

When you choose an object, you *focus* on a *specific idea*. You can see that your focus is an *example* for your general idea.

General topic ⟶ Focus

When you have a focus, you can begin the writing process.

FOCUS Using the Writing Process

Look at the steps that Hesham, a student from Egypt, followed when he wrote his composition.

General topic: a common object in my country
Focus: a coffee pourer

Step 1: Generating Ideas

Hesham wrote down all of his ideas.

used to serve coffee to guests
pretty
made of metal, usually brass
the brass is carved
curved body
narrow neck
handle
the cover is pointed
spout is long and thin

Step 2: Organizing Ideas

Hesham put his ideas into two groups. He put his general ideas into one group. He put the words that name the parts of the coffee pourer into another group.

General Ideas	*Parts*
used to serve coffee to guests	*body*
pretty	*neck*
	handle
	spout
	top

Then he organized the names of the parts of the coffee pourer. Look at this list of parts. What order did he use to name the parts of the coffee pourer?

Parts
1. body
2. neck
3. top
4. handle
5. spout

Hesham described the coffee pourer from *bottom to top*. When you describe an object, you can describe it in four possible ways.

1. From bottom to top
2. From top to bottom
3. From inside to outside
4. From outside to inside

The order that you choose should fit the object that you are describing. It is important to choose one specific way. Then your ideas will be in logical order.

> Logical order is any arrangement that is easy to follow and easy to understand. It can be any natural order.

Hesham organized his ideas. Then he decided that he needed more information. He wanted to describe the parts of the coffee pourer more specifically. He wrote down some more ideas. (He returned to Step 1: Generating ideas.)

> generate ideas ⟶ organize ⟶ generate more ideas

Here are the ideas that Hesham added to his description.

1. body: wide at the bottom
   narrow in the middle
   made of brass
   decorated with carved flowers
2. neck: above the body
   curved
   narrow

3. *top: becomes thinner as you go up*
graceful
pointed

4. *handle: attached to the top and the body*
curved

5. *spout: shaped like a crescent moon*
long and thin

Step 3: Writing the First Draft

When you write your first draft, it is important to get your ideas on paper. Do not worry about mistakes in grammar or punctuation. You can correct these mistakes later, in Focus: Proofreading Symbols.

FOCUS Logical Order

These sentences describe a flower. Look at the picture. Then put the sentences in order so that they describe a flower from bottom to top. When you finish, compare your answers with a classmate's.

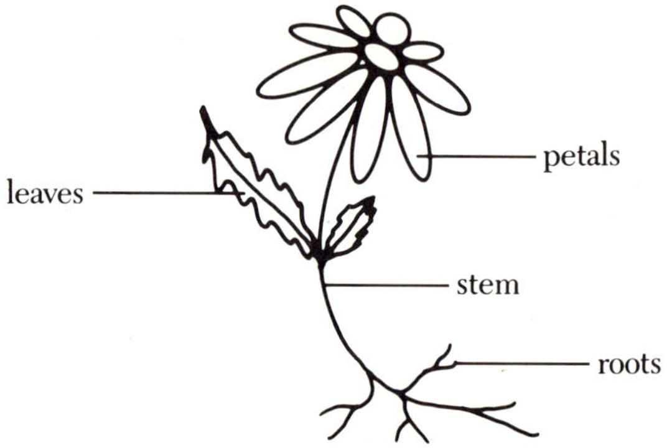

1. The stem is long and thin.
2. The petals give the flower its color and shape.
3. The roots are under the ground.
4. The leaves are usually green.

Exercise E: Logical Order Write four sentences describing an apple. Order your sentences to describe the apple from outside to inside.

Step 4: Revising

Here is the second paragraph of Hesham's composition about coffee pourers. It is from his first draft. You will see that some of the sentences are not in logical order. Work with a classmate. Put the sentences in logical order from bottom to top. Look at page 27 to be sure of the correct order.

(1) Most coffee pourers are made of brass. (2) The body is decorated with carved flowers. (3) The neck is above the body. (4) The body is wide at the bottom and narrow at the middle. (5) It is narrow and curved. (6) The handle is attached to the top and the body. (7) The spout is long and thin. (8) It is shaped like a crescent moon. (9) The top of the coffee pourer is very graceful. (10) There is a pointed decoration on top. (11) It is curved.

Step 5: Rewriting

Here is the second draft of the composition.

Most coffee pourers are made of brass. The body is decorated with carved flowers. The body is wide at the bottom and narrow at the middle. The neck is above the body. It is narrow and curved. The top of the coffee pourer is very graceful. There is a pointed decoration on top. The handle is attached to the top and the body. It is curved. The spout is long and thin. It is shaped like a crescent moon.

FOCUS Writing an Introduction

After you write your first draft, you will have a clear idea of what your topic is. You can now write an introduction to your composition.

First, the introduction tells what your topic is and what your focus is. Second, the introduction gives the reader some general information about your topic.

To write the introduction, use the general ideas. For example, look again at Hesham's general ideas.

General Ideas
used to serve coffee to guests
it is pretty
keeps the coffee hot

Now look at Hesham's complete composition. The first paragraph is his introduction.

A coffee pourer is a common object in Egypt. We like to have guests in our homes and we usually serve coffee to them. We like to use special coffee pourers because they are pretty. They also keep the coffee hot.

Most coffee pourers are made of brass. The body is decorated with carved flowers. The body is wide at the bottom and narrow at the middle. The neck is above the body. It is narrow and curved. The top of the coffee pourer is very graceful. There is a pointed decoration on top. The handle is attached to the top and the body. It is curved. The spout is long and thin. It is shaped like a crescent moon.

Things to Look at and Discuss

1. How many paragraphs does this composition have?
2. What is the job of the first paragraph?
3. What is the job of the second paragraph?
4. This composition describes the coffee pourer from bottom to top. Could you also describe it from top to bottom? Why or why not?

FOCUS Proofreading Symbols

You have already learned four proofreading symbols. Here is a new symbol for you to learn: **agr**.

agr You have a mistake in agreement.

1. subject-verb agreement

   Examples: He like (agr) chocolate very much.

   They is (agr) good students.

2. singular-plural agreement

   Examples: I have many friend (agr).

   I saw two film (agr) last week.

Exercise F: Proofreading for Agreement: Use the proofreading symbol **agr** to correct the mistakes in these sentences.

1. Hesham like to invite his friends to his home.

2. He often serve coffee to them.

3. There are many kind of coffee pourer.

4. Last week Hesham served coffee and dessert to five guest.

Exercise G: Some of these sentences have agreement mistakes. Find the mistakes and correct them.

1. John like the stained glass window in his living room.

2. It have blue and green rectangular panels around the outside.

3. The center have many oval piece of blue glass.

4. Around the center there is four green pieces of glass.

5. The frame is made of wood.

Here is a review of the five proofreading symbols that you now know.

cap	You need a capital letter.
p	You have a punctuation mistake.
sp	You have a spelling mistake.
¶	Make a new paragraph. Indent.
agr	You have a mistake in agreement.

Exercise H: Use the symbols to correct this paragraph. Rewrite the paragraph.

sp *cap*

Yesterday, I saw a beautiful sweater. I hope that I can by it! it is a

agr *cap* *agr*

heavy, blue knit with four button, the buttons is made of leather

p *p*

____

____

Exercise I: Correct the five mistakes in this paragraph. Then rewrite the paragraph.

This sweater will look beautiful with my plaid skirt the skirt is blue like the sweater it even have the same kind of buttons.

____

____

Step 6: Choosing a Title

Think of some possible titles for Hesham's composition. Discuss them with a classmate.

Writing Assignment

Choose one of these topics for a composition.

1. Describe a common object in your country.
2. Describe something that you would like to receive as a gift.
3. Imagine you are a mechanic or a carpenter. Describe a special tool or instrument that you use for work.
4. Describe some beautiful object in your home.

Follow these steps:

1. Discuss your topic with a classmate.
2. Write down your ideas. Check the spelling of your words.
3. Write your first draft.
4. Revise your first draft. Make sure your ideas are clear and in logical order.
5. Rewrite.
6. Proofread. Follow the checklist below.
7. Choose a title.

Proofreading Checklist

Proofread for each type of mistake, one by one. When you finish proofreading for each point on the list, put a check mark (✔) in the space.

1. _______ Did I give my composition a title?
2. _______ Did I write the title with capital letters?
3. _______ Did I indent every new paragraph?
4. _______ Did I begin each sentence with a capital letter?
5. _______ Did I put a period at the end of every sentence?
6. _______ Did I use correct subject-verb agreement?
7. _______ Did I check my spelling?

Lesson Four
Describing a Place

Introduction

When you describe a place, you want to give the reader a clear picture of that place. You want the reader to feel that he or she knows the place that you are describing.

A physical description of the place is part of this picture. You need to tell what the place looks like. For example, you can explain what kinds of things are in that place.

Another way to describe a place is to tell what people do there. Is this a place where people work, relax, or play sports? Or is it an important historical place?

All of this information will help the reader "see" what you are trying to describe.

FOCUS Punctuation—Using the Colon

We use the colon (:) when we have a list of more than two things in a sentence. We use commas between the items in the list. We use *and* before the last word in the list.

Example: The flowers are many colors: red, yellow, white, and blue.

Note: We never use a colon after a verb or after a preposition. For example, compare these sentences.

1. John went to the store and bought these things: apples, pears, and milk.
2. John went to the store and bought apples, pears, and milk.
3. John went to the store for apples, pears, and milk.

Exercise A: Punctuate these sentences.

1. You need these ingredients to make a cheese omelet eggs cheese milk onions butter salt and pepper
2. I am taking five subjects this semester English chemistry math political science and history
3. My three good friends are Shoji Mohammed and Raul
4. I have lived in these cities New York Denver Washington and Cairo
5. I have lived in New York Denver Washington and Cairo
6. The students in my English class are from these countries Japan Venezuela Kuwait Russia Korea and Saudi Arabia

Exercise B: Complete and punctuate these sentences.

1. There are three languages that are important to know ____________

____

2. These are the names of my teachers this year ____________________

____

3. These are three countries that I want to visit ______________________

____

4. There are three places in my country that every tourist should visit ____

5. Some popular sports in my country are ______________________

____

FOCUS Choosing a Topic

Suppose you want to describe a place in your country. That is your general topic.

Now you must focus on a specific place. Here are some ideas that will help you to choose which place you want to describe.

1. Choose a place that you like. You may not enjoy writing about a place that you don't like.
2. Choose a place that you know well.
3. Choose a place that other people will find interesting.

FOCUS Using the Writing Process

Here are the steps that Amina, a student from Oman, followed when she wrote her composition.

General topic: a place in my country
Focus: Rezat, a place that I like very much

Step 1: Generating Ideas

A good way to get some ideas is to talk about your topic with a classmate. Your classmate can ask you questions about your topic. Your discussion will help you get some ideas. Then you can write them down.

Amina's ideas are listed on the next page.

Rezat, a place I like very much

big
in the south
very green
many colors in the flowers: red, yellow, blue
many shapes
trees
caves with chairs inside
beautiful place
mountains
swimming pool
small river
farm
fruit
garden
people come on Friday
picnic in caves

Step 2: Organizing Ideas
Amina looked at her ideas. She saw that some of the ideas belonged together. She put her ideas into three groups. Then, she gave each group a name.

Exercise C: Put each of Amina's ideas into the correct group.

General Ideas	*What the Place Has*	*What People Do There*
big	*flowers*	*visit the caves*
beautiful	*trees*	

Step 3: Writing the First Draft
Amina used her groups of ideas to write the first draft. She used the general ideas for the first paragraph. She used the ideas in the second group for her second paragraph. She used the ideas in the third group for the third paragraph. Here is the first draft. You will see some mistakes in grammar, spelling, and punctuation. Don't worry about these mistakes. You will correct them in Focus: Proofreading Symbols (p. 47).

Rezat is a place in my country, Oman. I like it very much. It is a very nice place. It is big. It in the south. it is very green.

This place have a garden with many flower and many tree. The flowers is many colors: red, yellow, blue, and white. The trees is many colors: green and yellow. There is a swimming pool. There is a small river. There are many mountains. There is a farm with a lot of fruit.

This place has many caves. They are very good because

the gevernment put inside the caves chairs for the people. If he have a picnic, he can sit in that chairs. Many people come to this place on Friday because it a holiday. People like this place very much.

Step 4: Revising the First Draft

FOCUS Organization—Combining Sentences with the Same Topic

Here is Amina's first paragraph with the sentences numbered.

(1) Rezat is a place in my country. (2) I like it very much. (3) It is a very nice place. (4) It is big. (5) It is in the south. (6) It is very green.

This paragraph gives us the following information:

1. The name of the place
2. Where it is located
3. How the writer feels about it
4. What it looks like

Which sentences give us this information?

1. The name of the place *sentence 1*
2. Where it is located *sentences 1 and 5*
3. How the writer feels about it ______
4. What it looks like ______

Sentences 1 and 5 both give the location of Rezat. Both sentences have the same topic. These two sentences should be together in the paragraph. Here is the revised paragraph.

Rezat is a place in the south of my country. I like it very much. It is a nice place. It is big. It is very green.

FOCUS Combining Sentences by Putting Adjectives before the Noun

An adjective is a word that describes, or changes, or limits the meaning of a noun. Look at these sentences. We can combine each pair. We get a clearer description of the place when we put adjectives before the noun.

1. It is a very nice place. It is big.
   It is a very nice, big place.
2. It has mountains around it. The mountains are green.
   It has green mountains around it.

Exercise D: Combine each pair of sentences. Put the adjectives before the noun. If there are two adjectives, put a comma between those where one is needed.

1. New York is a busy city. It is a crowded city.

   ____

2. There are many trees in the park. They are green.

   ____

3. Jones Beach has beautiful sand. It is very soft.

   ____

4. This garden is a quiet place. It is a peaceful place.

   ____

5. Cherries is a disco. It is very lively.

   ____

6. An ant is an insect. It is very tiny.

7. Our classroom is a large room. It is rectangular.

8. An apple is a fruit. It is round. It is red.

9. There is a box for you on the table. The box is large. It is rectangular.

10. John has a kitten. It is cute. It is little.

FOCUS Combining Sentences by Using *and*

When two sentences have the same subject, we can put them together. We don't repeat the subject. We don't repeat the verb. Look at these examples.

1. It is round. It is very green.
   It is round and very green.

2. It has a swimming pool. It has a small river.
   It has a swimming pool and a small river.

3. This farm has many fruits. It has a garden.
   This farm has many fruits and a garden.

Exercise E: Combine each pair of sentences using *and*.

1. The flower is tall. It is beautiful.

____

2. My pencil is yellow. It is long.

____

3. My shoes are old. They are very comfortable.

____

4. John is tall. He is handsome.

____

5. New York is busy. It is crowded.

____

6. This park has a swimming pool. It has a small lake.

____

7. I am studying grammar. I am studying writing.

____

8. The package is large. It is square.

____

9. Washington Park is very big. It is rectangular.

____

10. He is rich. He is famous.

____

Exercise F: More Practice with Sentence Combining Read the following paragraph. Then rewrite it. Combine some sentences to make the paragraph more interesting.

One of my favorite places in Egypt is a resort town called Sharm El-Sheikh. It is a small town. It is on the Red Sea in the Sinai. I learned to scuba dive there. The water is very beautiful. It is warm and clear. You can see exquisite coral. You can see millions of fish. The fish are very colorful.

____

____

____

____

____

____

FOCUS Making Sure Your Sentences Are Correct

It is important to be sure that your sentences are correct. You want them to be accurate. Choose your words carefully. For example, look at this sentence from the composition.

Also, the trees are many colors: green and yellow.

Is the word *many* correct? Are green and yellow many colors? How can you change this sentence to make it more accurate? Write a better sentence here.

____

Step 5: Rewriting

Amina made many revisions in her composition. She put related sentences together. She combined some short sentences. She made sure her sentences were accurate.

Here are the first draft and the revised draft of the first two paragraphs. Compare each pair of paragraphs. See what kind of changes she made. For each pair of paragraphs, tell if she

1. Put related sentences together.
2. Combined short sentences with *and*.
3. Combined sentences by putting the adjectives before the noun.
4. Made her sentences more accurate.

First draft, first paragraph

Rezat is a place in my country, Oman. I like it very much. It is a very nice place. It is big. It in the south. it is very green

First draft, second paragraph

This place have a garden with many flower and many tree. The flowers is many colors: red, yellow, blue, and white. The trees is many colors: green and yellow. There is a swimming pool. There is a small river. There are many mountains. There is a farm with a lot of fruit.

Second draft, first paragraph

Rezat is a place in the south of my country, Oman. I like it very much. It is a nice, big place. It is very green.

Second draft, second paragraph

This place have a garden with many flower and many tree. The flowers is many colors: red, yellow, blue and white. The trees are green and yellow. There is a swimming pool and a small river. There are many mountains and a farm with a lot of fruit.

Exercise G: Practice with Revision Revise this paragraph. Improve the organization. Combine some sentences to make them longer and more interesting.

There is one place in New York that I like very much. It is called the Cloisters. It is a museum. It is in the middle of a park. The park is very big. The Cloisters looks like an old castle. It has stone walls. It is always cool inside. It is always quiet inside. Also, it has stone floors.

FOCUS Proofreading Symbols

You have already learned five proofreading symbols. Here are two new symbols: **wo** and ^.

wo Wrong word order.

Example: He speaks very well English. (*wo* above "very well")

Example: I bought a car new. (*wo* above "car new")

^ You forgot a word.

Example: He ^ a good friend.

Exercise H: These sentences come from Amina's composition. The proofreading symbols indicate the mistakes. Rewrite the sentences correctly.

1. It ^ in the south.

                                                                                    wo
2. They are very good because the government put <u>inside the cave chairs</u> for the people.

3. Many people come here on Friday because it^a holiday.

Exercise I: Now find and correct the mistakes yourself.

1. John a good artist.

2. He finished yesterday this picture.

3. It very beautiful.

Here is a list of the seven proofreading symbols you now know. Tell what they mean.

1. *cap* ______________________________

2. *p* ______________________________

3. *sp* ______________________________

4. ¶ ______________________________

5. *agr* ______________________________

6. *wo* ______________________________

7. ^ ______________________________

Exercise J: The proofreading symbols indicate mistakes in this paragraph. Rewrite the paragraph correctly.

                        agr   agr
This place have a garden with many flower and many tree. The

          agr   cap   agr
flowers is many colors: red, yellow, blue, and white. the trees is green^

yellow. There ^ a swimming pool and a small river ^ there are many

mountains and a farm with a lot of fruit.

Exercise K: Find and correct the mistakes in these paragraphs.

1. There are eight mistakes in this paragraph.

Rezat is a place in my country, oman. it in the south. I like it very much it is a nice big place it is very green.

2. There are seven mistakes in this paragraph.

This place has many caves. They are very good because the gevernment put inside the caves chairs for the people. If he have a picnic, he can sit in that chairs. Many people come here on Friday because it a holiday People like this place very much.

Step 6: Choosing a Title

The title is the first thing your reader sees. The title should be interesting. It should focus on your topic. It should not be too long.

Here are some possible titles for the composition that we read. Which titles do you like? Why? Discuss the titles in class.

1. Rezat
2. A Beautiful Place in My Country
3. A Good Place for a Picnic
4. A Special Place
5. A Place in My Country That I Like Very Much

Writing Assignment

Many governments want more tourists or business people to come to their countries. Imagine that you work for the government of your country. Your job is to write an advertisement for your country. The advertisement will make people want to visit your country, either for tourism or for business people.

Describe *one* place for tourists or *one* place for business people. Be specific. Do not describe your country in general.

Follow these steps:

1. Discuss your topic with a classmate. What are some questions you can ask your classmate about his or her topic? Here are a few suggestions. Work with your class and teacher to write some more.
   Where is the place located in your country?
   Why is it important?
   Do many tourists go there?
   What does it look like?
2. Write down your ideas.
3. Write your first draft.
4. Revise your first draft. Check your organization and information.
5. Rewrite.
6. Proofread. Follow the checklist on the next page.
7. Choose a title.

Proofreading Checklist

Proofread for each type of mistake, one by one. When you finish proofreading for each point on the list, put a check mark (✔) in the space.

1. _______ Did I give my composition a title?
2. _______ Did I write the title with capital letters?
3. _______ Did I indent every new paragraph?
4. _______ Did I begin each sentence with a capital letter?
5. _______ Did I put a period at the end of every sentence?
6. _______ Did I use correct subject-verb agreement?
7. _______ Did I check my spelling?
8. _______ Does every sentence have a subject and a verb?
9. _______ Did I use correct singular-plural agreement?
10. _______ Is my word order correct?

Lesson Five
Describing a Person

Introduction

When you describe someone, you want to give your reader a clear picture of that person. You want the reader to feel that he or she knows the person that you are describing.

A description of the person's physical appearance (what the person looks like) is part of your "picture." Here are some points that you may want to include in your physical description. Can you think of some others? Write them down here.

height
weight
hair color: black, brown, red, blond
hair length: long, medium length, short

____

____

____

____

____

Of course, what a person looks like is only a small part of the picture. You also want to tell the reader what kind of person you are describing. You can use adjectives to explain what this person is like. Here are a few adjectives that you can use to describe a person's personality. Can you think of some more? Write them down here.

kind
thoughtful
considerate
stubborn

Physical description and personality give your reader a very good picture of the person that you are describing. You can also add some more information. For example, you might describe the person's hobbies (things he or she likes to do) or talents (things this person does well). Here are some popular hobbies and talents.

Hobbies	*Talents*
I like dancing.	I am a good dancer.
I like singing.	I am a good singer.
I like playing tennis.	I am a good tennis player.

What are some others? Write them down here.

FOCUS Connecting Words to Add Information

Connecting words are important words for writing. We use connecting words to show that two sentences are related. There are many kinds of connecting words. One group of connectors is used to add more information about the same topic. Here are three connectors from that group.

furthermore
in addition
moreover

They have the same meaning as *and*.

Here are some examples of how we use these connectors.

1. John is a very good student. He comes to class every day. He always does his homework. **In addition,** he studies hard for all his tests.
2. My home town is New York. Many people are afraid of New York because they think it is a dangerous city. Some parts of New York are dangerous, but I think it is a wonderful city anyway. There is so much to do in New York. There are excellent restaurants and nightclubs. The discos are very exciting. **Moreover,** the shopping is excellent.

We don't use connectors for every sentence. Usually one or two connectors in a paragraph are enough.

FOCUS Punctuation

Furthermore, in addition, and **moreover** all follow the same punctuation rules. There are two ways to punctuate these words. The first way is to begin a new sentence with one of these words.

____________ . Furthermore, ________________________.

____________ . Moreover, __________________________.

____________ . In addition, ________________________.

period capital letter comma period

Example: He always does his homework. Furthermore, he always comes to school on time.

The second way to punctuate these words is to connect the two sentences with a semicolon (;). A semicolon is a special punctuation mark. It connects two complete sentences. A period puts a "stop" at the end of a sentence, but a semicolon is different. It shows your reader that your two sentences are closely related. When you use a semicolon, it is usually with connecting words like these below:

__________ ; furthermore, ____________________ .

__________ ; moreover, ____________________ .

__________ ; in addition, ____________________ .

Example: He always comes to school on time; furthermore, he is never absent.

Exercise A: Punctuate the following sentences. Be careful to use the period and semicolon correctly.

1. Mary is a kind, considerate person. She is always ready to help her friends in addition she is always willing to help a stranger.
2. Montana is a beautiful state. The mountains are very beautiful. There are many lakes and rivers In addition there are many national parks to visit.
3. English is not easy for me. I think that the grammar is confusing, and the pronunciation is difficult moreover the spelling is very difficult.
4. I worked very hard last night. I spent three hours doing my home-

work, and then cooked dinner furthermore I cleaned my whole apartment.

FOCUS Using the Writing Process

Step 1: Generating Ideas

In the last lesson you saw one way of generating ideas: making a list. Another way to generate and organize your ideas is to make a diagram. Put your main topic in the center of a circle. Use lines coming from this circle for your examples. You also can have more lines come out of your examples for more specific examples.

Here is an example of this kind of diagram. A student from Saudi Arabia chose this topic: describe an important person in your life. He decided to describe his wife.

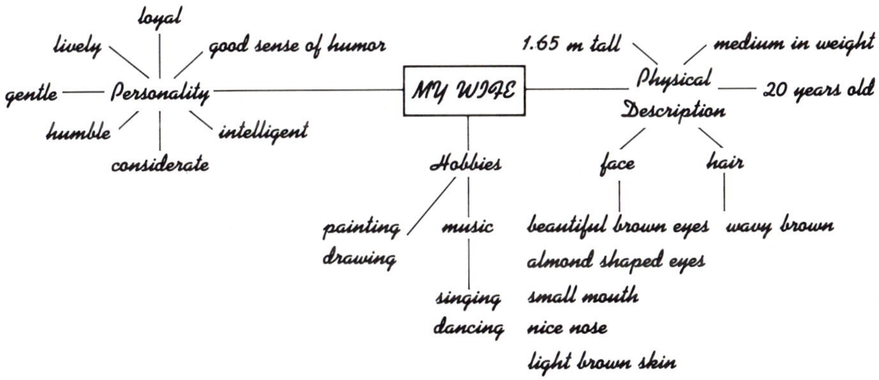

Step 2: Organizing Ideas

You can see that using a diagram will help you to organize your ideas. The diagram helps you keep related ideas together. Look again at the diagram above. Do you see that all of the words that describe the personality are together? All the words that give a physical description are together. All the words describing the hobbies are together. This kind of diagram is very helpful when you write your composition.

Step 3: Writing the First Draft

Here is the first draft of the composition.

My wife has a beautiful face. She has brown eyes. They are almond shaped, and she has a nice nose. She has wavy brown hair and light brown skin. She is twenty years old. She is medium in weight and she is one meter and 65 centimeters tall She is gentle and lively and considerate and she has a good sense of humor. She loves to laugh. She is intelligent and humble. She is loyal to me and her friends. She has several hobbies. American music, singing, dancing. She likes to paint and draw. I feel very lucky to have a wife like this. she makes my life wonderful.

Things to Look at and Discuss

1. Divide this composition into paragraphs. Where should each new paragraph begin? Why?
2. There are several places where this composition can be revised:
   The composition needs a short, general introduction. The introduction should tell the reader what the topic of the composition is.
   Some sentences can be combined to make them more interesting.
   The writer uses the word *and* a great deal. Different connectors should be used.
   Some words can be changed to make the composition more interesting.

Step 4: Revising

Look at the rough draft again. You can see that the writer made a number of comments and revisions *right on the rough draft.* This is an excellent way to begin revising your work. First, make some changes right on the rough draft. Then rewrite it.

My wife is an important person in my life. When I wake up I see My wife has a beautiful face. She has brown ^almond-shaped eyes.

~~They are almond shaped,~~ and ~~she has~~ a nice nose. She has wavy brown hair and light brown skin. She is twenty years old. She is medium in weight and ~~she is~~ one meter and 65 centimeters tall.

It is difficult to describe her personality. She is gentle and lively and considerate ~~and~~ moreover she has a good sense of humor. She loves to laugh. She is intelligent and humble. Finally, She is loyal to me and her friends.

She has several hobbies. American music, singing, dancing. She likes to paint and draw. I feel very lucky to have a wife like this. she makes my life wonderful.

Now look at the final draft. You will notice a few more changes. Discuss these changes with your classmates.

An Important Person in My Life

My wife is a very important person in my life. When I wake up in the morning, I see a beautiful face. She has brown, almond shaped eyes, a small mouth and a nice nose. In addition, she has wavy, brown hair and light brown skin. She is twenty years old. She is medium in weight and one meter and 65 centimeters tall.

It is difficult to describe everything about my wife's personality. When anybody talks with her, he can see her gentleness. Moreover, she is a lively, considerate person with a good sense of humor. She loves to laugh. She is intelligent and humble. Finally, she is loyal to me and her friends.

My wife has several hobbies. She likes American music, singing, and dancing. In addition, she likes to paint and draw. I feel very lucky to have a wife like this. She makes my life wonderful.

Things to Look at and Discuss

1. What is the focus of the first paragraph? Do all of the sentences talk about this idea? Does each sentence add something new and important? Do all of the sentences fit together?
2. What is the topic of the second paragraph? Which sentence is the topic sentence? What are some examples for this topic?
3. What connecting word is used in the third paragraph? Why was it used? Was it used correctly?

Exercise B: Practice with Revision Here is the first draft of a composition written by another student. It is about the student's mother.

My Mother

I have someone that I love a lot. She is my mother. She is very patient with me. She helps me when I have a problem.

My mother is a very understanding, sensitive woman. She has good sense. She is forty-three years old. She has black hair, brown eyes, ruddy skin, straight hair, and she is tall also.

In addition, she is an elementary school teacher. My mother taught me how I should be in life because life is hard, you have to look for your happiness and luck. My experiences are few because I am very young, too, but I have learned from her. My mother is the best in the world.

This composition has several good points. It is interesting. It has some good examples and good vocabulary. However, the organization is not very good.

Answer these questions about the composition. The answers will help you to improve the organization.

1. The first two sentences of this composition are the introduction. What is the focus of the next two sentences?
2. Look at the second paragraph. What is the focus of the first sentence? Do the other sentences in this paragraph have the same focus? Should these sentences all be in the same paragraph? Can you put the first sentence in a different place? Where does it belong?
3. Look at the last paragraph. Which sentence doesn't belong?

Step 5: Rewriting
Here is the composition again. Look at the comments that the teacher wrote. Use the answers to the questions above and the teacher's comments. Revise and rewrite the composition. When you finish, compare your rewrite with a classmate's.

My Mother

I have someone that I love a lot. She is my mother. She is very patient with me. She helps me when I have a problem.

My mother is a very understanding, sensitive woman. She has good sense. She is forty-three years old. She has black hair, brown eyes, ruddy skin, straight hair, and she is tall also.

combine

is this word necessary?

same ¶?

In addition, she is an elementary school teacher. My mother taught me how I should be in life because life is hard, you have to look for your happiness and luck. My experiences are few because I am very young, too, but I have learned from her. My mother is the best in the world.

does this sentence belong?

omit

____

____

____

____

____

____

____

____

____

____

____

____

FOCUS Proofreading Symbols

You have already learned six proofreading symbols. Do you remember what they are? Write the correct symbol in each space.

1. ______________ You need a capital letter.
2. ______________ You have a mistake in punctuation.
3. ______________ You have a spelling mistake.
4. ______________ Make a new paragraph. Indent.

5. ______________ Incorrect agreement.

6. ______________ You forgot a word.

Here is a new symbol for you to learn: **wf**.

wf Wrong form of the word.

Examples: She is a beauty girl. (wf above "beauty")

He runs quick. (wf above "quick")

Let's look more closely at some other examples.

FOCUS Adverbs

An adverb is a word or phrase that changes, describes, or limits the meaning of a verb, an adjective, or another adverb. Some adverbs add information about verbs. Most verbs describe actions (go, put, walk). Adverbs add information about these actions by answering certain questions.

Examples:
1. Carlos and Marta began to talk seriously about marriage.
   How did they talk?
   They began to talk *seriously*.
2. Kei and Rika want to get married soon.
   When do they want to get married?
   They want to get married *soon*.

Some adverbs add information about adjectives. These adverbs answer the question *how much*.

Example: I promise to be *very* careful.

Adverbs that answer the question *how* usually end in -ly. You can often form these adverbs by adding -ly to an adjective.

Examples:
1. He is a *serious* student. He works *seriously*.
2. He is a *polite* person. He speaks *politely*.

Exercise C: Circle the correct form from each pair of words in the parentheses.

1. Maria wants to be a professional singer. I think she will be (successful, successfully). She certainly sings (beautiful, beautifully).
2. The rain fell (heavily, heavy). I listened as it made (loud, loudly) noises on the window will. I could see that the streets were (quick, quickly) becoming full of water.

Exercise D: The proofreading symbol **wf** indicates mistakes in this paragraph. Rewrite the paragraph correctly.

Ali is an excellent student. All of his teachers like him very much. He studies hard and always does him (wf) homework. In addition, he is always politely (wf) in class.

Exercise E: Use all seven symbols to correct the mistakes in this paragraph.

Ellen my best frend. I have known her since we were ten year old. she is a very kind sensitively person. In addition, she intelligent, and she have a good sense of humor.

Exercise F: There are 18 mistakes in this paragraph. Find the mistakes and correct the paragraph.

Fardooz live in Casablana Morocco. she have two son. one son two years old. the other son is six he go to school Fardooz work very hard she work for my friend. she is honestly and very reliable.

Step 6: Choosing a Title

The Saudi student chose the title "An Important Person in My Life" for his composition. The other student chose the title "My Mother" for her composition. Which title do you prefer? Why?

Writing Assignment

Choose one of these topics.

1. Describe the person you want to marry.
2. Describe an important person in your life.
3. Describe your best friend.
4. Describe your favorite teacher.
5. Describe someone who taught you an important lesson.
6. Describe someone who changed you in some way.

Follow these steps:

1. Talk about your topic with a classmate. What are some questions you might ask? Here are a few suggestions. Try to think of some more.
   Who are you going to write about?
   Why is this person important to you?
   What is this person like?
2. Draw a diagram like the one on page 57 for your ideas.
3. Write your first draft.
4. Check your organization and content. Make some comments right on your draft.
5. Revise.
6. Proofread. Follow the checklist below.
7. Choose a title.

Proofreading Checklist

Proofread for each type of mistake, one by one. When you finish proofreading for each point on the list, put a check mark (✔) in the space.

1. _______ Did I give my composition a title?
2. _______ Did I write the title with capital letters?
3. _______ Did I indent every new paragraph?
4. _______ Did I begin each sentence with a capital letter?
5. _______ Did I put a period at the end of every sentence?

6. ______ Did I use correct subject-verb agreement?

7. ______ Did I check my spelling?

8. ______ Does every sentence have a subject and a verb?

9. ______ Did I use correct singular-plural agreement?

10. ______ Is my word order correct?

11. ______ Is each word in the correct form?

Lesson Six

Narration

Introduction

In a narration, you tell a story. You can tell something that happened to you or that happened to another person. You can also make up (invent) a story.

Your job is to help the reader understand clearly what happened. You want the reader to feel that he or she was there, seeing the story take place. You might think of this as "making a movie" with your words.

FOCUS Connecting Words for Chronological Order

Chronological order means "time order." When you tell a story, you usually tell the events in the order in which they happened. You start at the beginning and go to the end.

Here are some connecting words you can use to help the reader understand the order of your story.

First, . . .	Usually used for the first event.
Next, . . .	Can be used for the second event.
Then, . . . **After that, . . .** **Afterward, . . .**	Can be used for the third, fourth, etc. Basically, they have the same meaning.
Later, . . .	For an event later in time.

Finally, . . .	For the last event in a series.
At the same time, . . .	For events that happened at the same time.

These connecting words all follow the same punctuation rule. They usually begin a new sentence, so you need to write them with a capital letter. We usually (but not always) put a comma after these words.

Here are some examples of how we use these connectors. You don't need a connector for every sentence. Furthermore, you don't need to use every connector on the list.

1. Yesterday was a busy day for me. **First,** I got up very early and got dressed. **Next,** I packed my bags. I ate a small breakfast: some fruit, some bread, and a cup of coffee. **Afterward,** I got into my car and drove to my parents' house. I visited with them for a few hours. **Later,** I got back into my car. I had to drive three hours to my new home in another city. **Finally,** I arrived at my new apartment.
2. Mr. Dull's life is not very interesting. He does the same thing every day. I don't know how he can stand it! **First,** he gets up at 7:00. He takes a shower, shaves, and gets dressed. He always puts on a dark suit, a white shirt, and a blue tie. **After that,** he has his breakfast and reads the paper. **Finally,** he is ready to leave for work at 8:15.

Exercise A: There is a space for a connector before every new sentence in the following paragraphs. Decide where you really need a connector. Decide which connector to use. *Do not put a connector in every space*. Put a connector where it is necessary. Then add the correct punctuation.

Moving from New York to Seattle wasn't easy. __________ there were so many things to do! __________ I had to find someone to take my apartment. __________________ I had to pack all my things. __________ that was a big job. __________ I had to decide what I could take with me and what I had to leave behind. __________ I had to say goodbye to my friends. __________ I guess that was the most difficult part. __________ I had to load up my car and drive three thousand miles by myself.

FOCUS Using the Writing Process

In the following composition, Minoru, a Japanese student, describes his last day in Japan before coming to the United States.

Step 1: Generating Ideas

Minoru wrote down some general ideas that would help him to describe that day.

What I did
How I felt
What my family did
How my family felt

Then he wrote down specific examples for his general ideas. He made a list like the one in Lesson 3.

What I Did
got up early
checked my baggage
checked my passport, ticket, travelers' checks
ate sushi
↖ went to a Japanese restaurant

How I Felt
excited
hopeful
terrified of flying
anxious that I might forget something
worried I might miss Japanese food

How My Family Felt
mother—serious
father—thoughtful
brother and sister-in-law—pleased

Things to Look at and Discuss

1. Notice that in the first section, "What I did," Minoru added the information "went to a Japanese restaurant." He drew an arrow to show where this step belonged.
2. Notice that in this list he did *not* include "What my family did." He decided not to put that in the composition. Maybe he thought it wasn't necessary for the composition. Perhaps he decided it was not important. Maybe he didn't have enough to say about it.

Remember, *you can change your mind at any time during the writing process*. This is very important. You can add, change, or take out information any time you want. You can even change your topic if you don't like it. (Of course, then you have to begin again.)

Step 2: Organizing Ideas

Minoru connected his related ideas. He wanted to show the relationship between what he did and how he felt. He thought this was the best way to explain a very important day in his life.

What I Did		*How I Felt*
Got up early	→	*Excited, hopeful* *Terrified about flying*
Checked my baggage: passport, travelers' checks, tickets	→	*Anxious about forgetting something important*
Went to a Japanese restaurant. Ate sushi.	→	*Worried about missing Japanese food*

Step 3: Writing the First Draft

Use your notes to begin writing. Get your ideas on paper. Here is Minoru's first draft.

I got up early because I was excited. I was terrified about flying in an airplane across the ocean. This was my first trip to a new country, so I felt hopeful. I checked my baggage to see that my passport, travelers' checks and tickets were there. Then I went to a Japanese restaurant to eat sushi. My parents and brother felt many things, too. My mother was very serious. She would not see me for many months. My father was very thoughtful. My elder brother and his wife felt pleased I would bring them many gifts from America three months later. Now I am in America. Although America is a wonderful place to live, I miss Japan. I long for Japanese food, nature, my parents and friends. Everyone knows there is no place like home.

Step 4: Revising the First Draft

Here is the first draft with the notes, revisions, and comments that Minoru made on it. Making notes like this on your first draft can save you some time before you actually rewrite your composition.

First, ^ I got up early because I was excited. I was terrified about flying in an airplane across the ocean ^ for so many hours. This was my first trip to a new country, so I felt hopeful. ^ Next, I checked my baggage to see ~~that~~ if my passport, travelers' checks and tickets were there. Then I went to a Japanese restaurant to eat sushi. ^ (typical Japanese food—raw fish) My parents and brother felt many things, too. My mother was very serious. She would not see me for many months. My father was very thoughtful.

My elder brother and his wife felt pleased I would bring them many gifts from America. ~~three months later.~~ Now I am in America. Although America is a wonderful place to live, I miss Japan. I long for Japanese food, nature, my parents and friends. Everyone knows there is no place like home.

Minoru then wrote an introduction to his composition. As you learned in Lesson Three, the introduction should do the following.

1. tell what your topic is and what your focus is
2. give some general information about your topic

Here is Minoru's introduction.

I left Japan on March 11, 1984. I clearly remember how I felt and what I did on that day.

Things to Look at and Discuss

1. What is Minoru's general topic?
2. What is his focus?
3. What other information does his introduction give you?

Step 5: Rewriting

Now let's read Minoru's final draft.

I left Japan on March 11, 1984. I clearly remember what I did and how I felt on that day.

First, I got up early because I was excited. I was terrified about flying in an airplane across the ocean for so many hours. This was my first trip to a new country, so I also felt hopeful. Next, I checked my baggage to see if my passport, travelers' checks and tickets were there. Later, I realized I might miss

Japanese food. I went to a Japanese restaurant to eat sushi. This is a typical Japanese food made of raw fish.

At the same time my family felt many things. My mother was very serious. She would not see me for a long time. My father was thoughtful. My elder brother and his wife were pleased. I would bring them many gifts from America.

Now I am in America. Although America is a wonderful place, I miss Japan. I long for Japanese food, nature, my parents and friends. Everyone knows there is no place like home.

Things to Look at and Discuss

1. Look back at page 70, Step 2: Organizing Ideas. Look at the way Minoru connected his ideas. Then reread the second paragraph of his composition.

Exercise B: Find the sentences that tell *what Minoru did*. Underline them. Then write them down here.

1. ____

2. ____

3. ____

Now, find the sentences that tell *how Minoru felt*. Underline them. Then write them down here.

1. ____

2. ____

3. ____

Do you see how his organization works in his composition? Discuss this with your classmates.

2. When you write a narration, it is possible to describe just the action. You can explain in chronological order what happened.

Minoru told what he did that day in chronological order, but he also told how he felt. Why do you think he did that?

3. Reread the following paragraph from the composition.

First, I got up early because I was excited. I was terrified about flying in an airplane across the ocean for so many hours. This was my first trip to a foreign country, so I also felt hopeful. Next, I checked my baggage to see if my passport, travelers' checks and tickets were there. Later, I realized that I might miss Japanese food. I went to a Japanese restaurant to eat sushi. This is a typical Japanese food made of raw fish.

Exercise C: Find and underline these connectors in the above paragraph: **first, next, later.**

Which of the above connectors

1. introduces the first event in the series? ______________________
2. introduces the second event? ______________________________
3. introduces an event that happened later in time? ____________

FOCUS More Practice Writing Introductions

Writing an introduction is difficult for many students. It is important to make your introduction general, but it should not be too general. It should focus on your topic. In this way, the reader has an idea of what you are writing about.

Look at these sentences from another student's introduction.

Everybody is sad to leave his or her home and go to a new place.

Is this sentence true? Is it correct? Is **everybody** sad to leave his or her home and go to a new place? Aren't many people happy to go to a new place?

It is always difficult to leave your friends and family.

Do you agree with this sentence? Is it **always** difficult to leave?

These sentences are too general. They are not true because they are too general. Be careful about using these words in your introduction: *always, never, everyone, everybody, nobody*. They are usually too general.

Here is the same introduction. Look at the changes that the student made. Discuss the changes with your classmates.

It ~~is always~~ can be difficult to leave your friends and family. ~~Everybody is sad~~ I was unhappy to leave ~~his or her~~ my home. The day that I left Kuwait was very sad for me.

FOCUS Proofreading Symbols

You have already learned eight proofreading symbols. Here is a new one: **tns**.

tns Wrong verb tense.

Example: He get (tns) a new car yesterday.

Example: I am going (tns) to school every day.

Exercise D: Look at this paragraph from Minoru's composition. Underline all the verbs in the paragraph.

I left Japan on March 11, 1984. I clearly remember what I did and how I felt on that day.

Answer these questions:

1. All of the verbs are in the past tense except one. Which verb is not in the past tense? Why?

2. Why are the other verbs in the past tense? When do we use the past tense?

____

Exercise E: Look at this paragraph. Underline the verbs.

Now, I am in America. Although America is a wonderful place to live, I miss Japan. I long for Japanese food, nature, my parents and friends. Everyone knows there is no place like home.

Answer these questions:

1. What tense are these verbs in?

____

2. Why?

____

3. Why is the tense in this paragraph different from most of the verbs in the other paragraphs? Which word tells you to change the verb tense? Which word tells you that the *time* in the last paragraph is different from the rest of the composition?

____

Exercise F: This paragraph has some mistakes in verb tense. The mistakes are marked with the proofreading symbol **tns.** Correct the mistakes.

When I got off the plane in Cairo, I am (tns) very surprised by what I see (tns). I knew for certain that I was in a foreign country. Men are (tns) wearing long robes and turbans. People are (tns) speaking loudly in Arabic. I couldn't understand a word. I nervously begin to look around for my husband.

Exercise G: This paragraph has some mistakes in the verb tense. First, underline all of the verbs. Then, correct the mistakes.

I have been in Cairo for three months. When I first arrived, everything seems strange to me. Now, I was not surprised when I see donkey carts in the streets. I don't notice that many of the men are wearing long robes. I even understood a little Arabic.

Step 6: Choosing a Title

Minoru chose this title for his composition:

"The Day I Left Japan"

Do you like this title? Why or why not?

Writing Assignment

Choose one of these topics for a composition.

1. Write about a wonderful experience. What happened? How did you feel?
2. Write about a terrible experience. What happened? How did you feel?
3. Write about an event that changed you in some way.
4. Write about a trip that you took.
5. Write about a story that is popular in your country.
6. Make up your own story.

Follow these steps:

1. Talk about your topic with a classmate. What are some questions

that you can ask your classmate? Work with your class and teacher to think of some questions.
2. Write down your ideas. Connect related ideas.
3. Write your first draft.
4. Exchange papers with a classmate. Read each other's papers. Make some suggestions to your classmate.
5. Revise your first draft. Check your introduction. Make sure your information is in chronological order.
6. Rewrite. Don't forget, you can add or take away any information you want.
7. Proofread. Follow the checklist below.
8. Choose a title.

Proofreading Checklist

Proofread for each type of mistake, one by one. When you finish proof-reading for each point on the list, put a check mark (✔) in the space.

1. ______ Did I give my composition a title?
2. ______ Did I write the title with capital letters?
3. ______ Did I indent every new paragraph?
4. ______ Did I begin each sentence with a capital letter?
5. ______ Did I put a period at the end of every sentence?
6. ______ Did I use correct subject-verb agreement?
7. ______ Did I check my spelling?
8. ______ Does every sentence have a subject and a verb?
9. ______ Did I use correct singular-plural agreement?
10. ______ Did I use correct word order?
11. ______ Is each word in the correct form?
12. ______ Did I use the correct verb tense?

Lesson Seven
Process

Introduction

When you explain a process, you explain *how* to do something. A process is a series of steps you must take to reach a certain result or goal. Usually, you must perform these steps in a specific order. Some processes are easy; for example, making tea normally requires a few basic steps. Other processes, such as building a house, are very complicated. One process that you already know very well is the process of writing a composition.

In order to explain any process, simple or complicated, it is necessary to include all the steps in **chronological order.** In addition, many of the steps will need some explanation. A simple list of steps is not enough to explain most processes.

FOCUS More Practice with Chronological Order

You can combine sentences with the word **after.** Look at these sentences.

After you fill out the forms, you will take the written test.

After you add the potatoes, you will cook the soup for twenty minutes.

After John eats dinner, he will do his homework.

Each of these sentences has two parts. Each part has a different action. In each sentence, which is the first action? Which is the second action?

Notice the verb tenses used in each part of the sentence. What tense is used for the first action? What tense is used for the second action?

FOCUS Punctuation

There are two ways to write this kind of sentence:

1. After you fill out the forms, you will take the written test.

   after — *first action* — comma — *second action*

2. You will take the written test after you fill out the forms.

   second action — after — *first action*

Exercise A: Punctuate each sentence as necessary.

1. After you arrive you will take the Michigan Test.
2. After you take the Michigan Test we will tell you what level you are in.
3. You can take the TOEFL after you know some more English.
4. After you take the TOEFL you will wait several weeks for your score.
5. You can apply to some universities after you get your score.

Exercise B: Combine each pair of sentences using **after.** Use the correct verb tenses and punctuation. Look at the example.

Example: Put the eggs in the bowl. Beat them with a fork.
After you put the eggs in a bowl, you will beat them with a fork.

1. Put some butter in the pan. Fry some onions for five minutes.

____

____

2. Pour the eggs into the pan. Add the cheese.

____

____

3. Cover the pan. Lower the heat.

____

____

4. Cook the omelet for five minutes. Check to see if it is ready.

____

____

5. Take the omelet out of the pan. Put it on a plate.

____

____

FOCUS Using the Writing Process

Getting a state driver's license is an important process for most people living in the United States. We will use this process to show you how to generate and organize your own ideas.

Step 1: Generating Ideas

Write down the main steps of the process.

1. Take the written test.
2. Take the eye exam.
3. Take the driving test.
4. Pay the fee.

Within each main step, there are several smaller steps. We can call these smaller steps *substeps*. Write down the important substeps for each main step.

Main Steps and Substeps

Take the written test	get the driver's manual study the laws go to the motor vehicle office go to the information desk take the written test give the written test to the clerk
Take the eye exam	
Take the driving test	
Pay the fee	the clerk takes your picture give the clerk your name and address pay the fee and get your license

Step 2: Organizing Ideas

An excellent way to organize the steps in a process is to use a diagram. A diagram can show the order of the steps you must follow. It can also show the order of any substeps.

This diagram shows the main steps and substeps for getting a state driver's license in the United States.

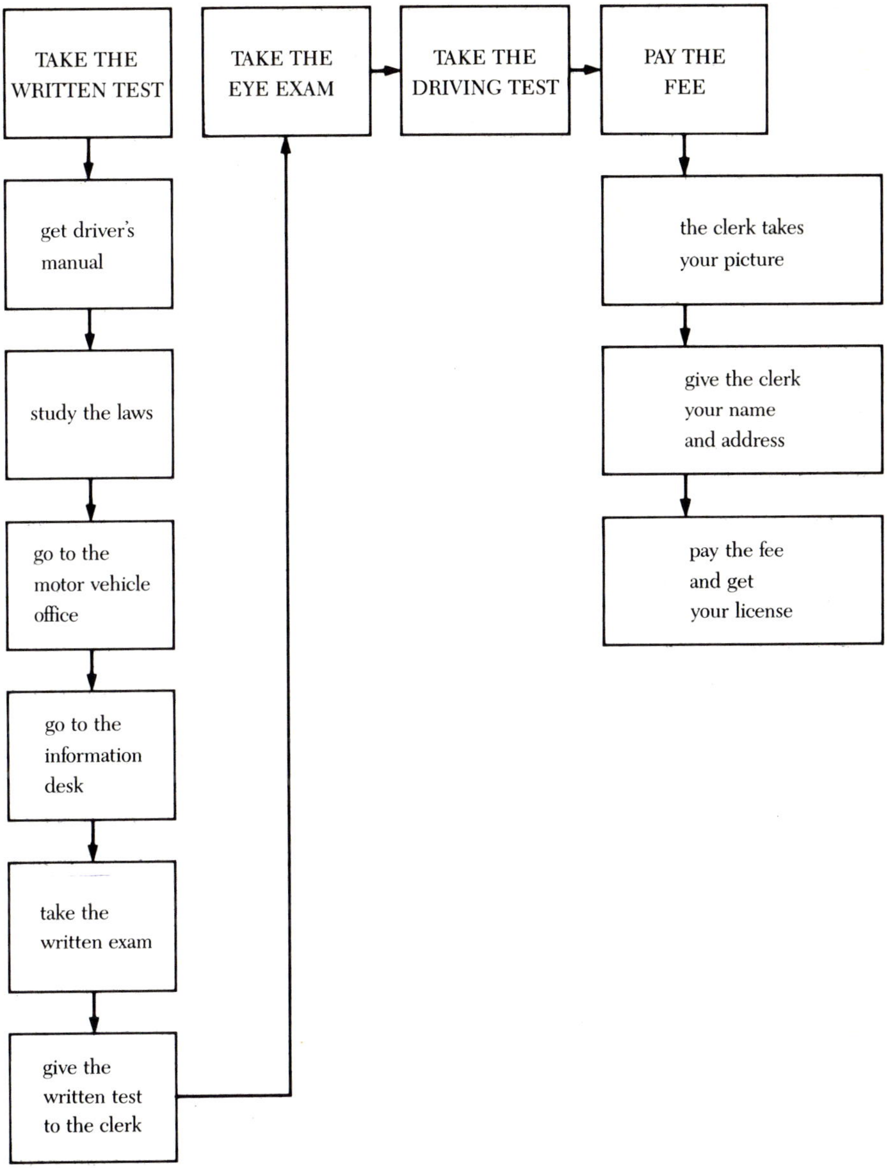
TAKE THE WRITTEN TEST
get driver's manual
study the laws
go to the motor vehicle office
go to the information desk
take the written exam
give the written test to the clerk
TAKE THE EYE EXAM
TAKE THE DRIVING TEST
PAY THE FEE
the clerk takes your picture
give the clerk your name and address
pay the fee and get your license

Step 3: Writing the First Draft

You can use a diagram to write your first draft. It will help you keep your ideas organized.

Here is the first draft of the composition. We will read it and revise it paragraph by paragraph. Because it is the first draft, you may see some mistakes in grammar and punctuation. You will correct these mistakes later in Focus: Proofreading Symbols.

Everyone needs a driver's license. It is important to have one. There are two test you have to take. You have to take a written test. You have to take a driving test.

You have to study for the written test. You can get a driver's manual. At any motor vehicle office. This manual give you all the information that you need to study.

When you know the information in the manual, go to the motor vehicle office. Stop at the information desk. Tell the clerk that you want to take the driver's license test. The clerk will give you some forms to fill out. You will fill out the forms. You will take the written test. Answer each question carefully. Give your test to the clerk. The clerk will correct the test and tell you if you pass.

If you pass the written test. You will take an eye exam. You will take the driving test. You must have your own car for the driving test.

If you pass the test. You will get your license. A clerk will take your picture. Another clerk will type your name and address on a card. You will pay the fee and get your license.

Things to Look at and Discuss

1. Look at the underlined parts of the composition. Then look back at the diagram on page 83. Did the information in the underlined areas come from the diagram? Where did this information come from?
2. It is common to get some more ideas while you are writing your first draft. Sometimes you get some of your best ideas while writing the first draft. Be sure to include them in your composition. Remember, you can add or take out any information when you write your first draft.

Step 4: Revising the First Draft

Exercise C: Work with a classmate. Revise the composition paragraph by paragraph. Use the instructions below to help you. Use a separate sheet of paper to rewrite.

Paragraph 1

(1) Everyone needs a driver's license. (2) It is important to have one. (3) There are two tests you have to take. (4) You have to take a written test. (5) You have to take a driving test.

1. Look at sentence 1. Is it true? Does everyone need a driver's license?
2. Combine sentences 3, 4, and 5. Use a colon.
3. Rewrite paragraph 1.

Paragraph 2

(1) You have to study for the written test. (2) You can get a driver's manual at any motor vehicle office. (3) This manual gives you all the information that you need to study.

1. Put a connecting word at the beginning of this paragraph.

2. Rewrite the paragraph. Put it after paragraph 1. Don't forget to indent.

Paragraph 3

(1) When you know the information in the manual, go to the motor vehicle office. (2) Stop at the information desk. (3) Tell the clerk that you want to take the driver's license test. (4) The clerk will give you some forms to fill out. (5) You will fill out the forms. (6) You will take the written test. (7) Answer each question carefully. (8) Give your test to the clerk. (9) The clerk will correct the test and tell you if you pass.

1. Put connecting words before sentence 2 and before sentence 3.
2. Combine sentences 5 and 6 using *after*.
3. Put a connecting word before sentence 8.

Paragraph 4

(1) If you pass the written test, you will take an eye exam. (2) You will take the driving test. (3) You must have your own car for the driving test.

1. Put a connecting word before sentence 2.

Paragraph 5

(1) If you pass the test, you will get your license. (2) A clerk will take your picture. (3) Another clerk will type your name and address on a card. (4) You will pay the fee and get your license.

1. Put connecting words before sentences 2, 3, and 4.

Step 5: Rewriting

Now compare your revision with the copy below. It may be a little different because every writer usually has different ideas.

How to Get Your State Driver's License

If you already know how to drive, it will be easy to get your state driver's license. There are two tests that you have to take: a written test and a driving test.

First, you have to study for the written test. You can get a driver's manual at any motor vehicle office. This manual gives you all the information that you need to study.

When you know the information in the manual, go to the motor vehicle office. First, stop at the information desk. Tell the clerk that you want to take the driver's license test. The clerk will give you some forms to fill out. After you fill out the forms, you will take the written test. Answer each question carefully. Then, give your test to the clerk. The clerk will correct the test and tell you if you pass.

If you pass the written test, you will take an eye exam. Then you will take the driving test. You must have your own car for the driving test.

If you pass the test, you will get your license. First, a clerk will take your picture. Then another clerk will type your name and address on a card. Finally, you will pay the fee and get your license.

Things to Look at and Discuss

1. Look at the first paragraph. What job does it do? Notice how direct it is. It is an introduction, but it goes directly to the topic. It names the topic in the very first sentence.
2. Look at the first sentence. "If *you* already know how to drive, it will be easy to get your state driver's license." Who is *you*? In English, when we are giving general instructions or information, we usually use *you* as the subject. Here, *you* means "everyone" or "people in general." It does not mean "you personally."
3. Go through the composition. Underline each connecting word. Discuss the use of the connecting words.
4. Use conditionals to explain the steps of a process. Look at these sentences:
   a. If you already know how to drive, it will be easy to get your driver's license.
   b. If you pass your written test, you will take an eye exam.
   c. If you pass the test, you will get your license.

Each of the sentences has two parts: a cause and a result. Here is sentence a.

If you already know how to drive, it will be easy to get your state driver's license.

cause — result

Which part is the cause and which part is the result for sentences b and c?

b. If you pass your written test, you will take an eye exam.
c. If you pass the test, you will get your license.

Notice the verb tenses used in each part of the sentences. What verb tense is used for the cause? What verb tense is used for the result?

FOCUS Punctuation

You can write this kind of sentence in two ways.

1. If you pass your written test, you will take an eye exam.

if	cause	comma	result
1	2	3	4

2. You will take an eye exam if you pass your written test.

result	if	cause
1	2	3

The only difference between the two sentences is the comma. The meaning is the same.

Exercise D: Fill in each space with the correct form of the verb in parentheses. Then add a comma if one is needed.

1. If you __________ (study) hard you __________ (get) good grades.
2. If you __________ (get) good grades your family __________ (be) pleased.
3. You __________ (be) unhappy if you __________ (do) badly in school.
4. If you __________ (practice) every day you __________ (learn) quickly.
5. You __________ (feel) more comfortable if you __________ (understand) English better.

FOCUS Proofreading Symbols

Here is a new, very important proofreading symbol: **frag.**

frag You do not have a complete sentence.

Frag is short for "fragment." A fragment is a small piece of something. Here are some examples of sentence fragments.

After it rains
If you eat too much
To school every day
At the supermarket

Look at the first draft of the composition on page 84. There are sentence fragments in paragraphs 2, 4, and 5. Find them and correct them.

There are other mistakes in the rough draft on page 84. See if you can find them.

1. Paragraph 1: Find the mistake in singular-plural agreement. Correct it.
2. Paragraph 2: Correct the mistake in subject-verb agreement.

Exercise E: Use proofreading symbols to correct the mistakes in this paragraph.

It easy to write a good composition. If you follow these steps. first, you need to deside what you want to write about. Write down all your ideas. Then, you must organize your ideas. after that you can write your first draft. After you will write the first draft you will make your revision.

Exercise F: Correct this paragraph.

The first draft the first copy of your composition. You will change this copy several times. Before you are finished.

Step 6: Choosing a Title

Here are the title and the first sentence of the composition that we read.

Title: How to Get Your State Driver's License
First sentence: If you already know how to drive, it will be easy to get your state driver's license.

Notice that both the title and the first sentence are very direct. They tell you the topic immediately. This directness is typical for describing a process. You write about a process to tell someone how to do something. The reader reads about the process because he or she wants to know how to do something. The reader does not want to waste time. He or she wants to know right away if your process has the information that is needed.

Your title should be clear and to the point. It should tell the reader exactly what process you are explaining.

There are two common ways to name your process in the title. These are examples.

1. How to Get Your State Driver's License
2. Getting Your State Driver's License

Exercise G: Change these titles with verb form **-ing** to titles with **How to.**

1. Operating a Telex Machine ____________________
2. Getting a Student Visa in South Korea ____________________
3. Making a Paper Kite ____________________
4. Repairing a Flat Tire ____________________

Writing Assignment

Choose a process to write about. Here are some suggestions. Perhaps you have other ideas. Be sure to choose a process that you know well.

1. Getting a passport in your country
2. Getting a driver's license in your country
3. Paying bills (such as a telephone or electricity bill) in your country
4. Getting married in your country
5. Operating some sort of machine
6. How to fix something

Follow these steps:

1. Explain the process to a classmate.
2. Write down the main steps of the process.
3. Write down the important substeps. Check a dictionary for special vocabulary. Ask your teacher for some vocabulary as well. Check your spelling, too.
4. Make a diagram. Be sure your steps are in chronological order.

5. Write the first draft.
6. Revise. Is your introduction direct and clear? Use connecting words that will help the reader.
7. Rewrite.
8. Proofread. Follow the checklist below.
9. Choose a title.
10. Exchange papers with a classmate. Check each other's compositions. Make sure everything is clear. Use the proofreading checklist below and proofread your classmate's paper. Use the proofreading symbols to correct any mistakes that you find.
11. Make any final changes in your paper and give it to your teacher.

Proofreading Checklist

Proofread for each type of mistake, one by one. When you finish proofreading for each point on the list, put a check mark (✔) in the space.

1. ______ Did I give my composition a title?
2. ______ Did I write the title with capital letters?
3. ______ Did I indent every new paragraph?
4. ______ Did I begin each sentence with a capital letter?
5. ______ Did I put a period at the end of every sentence?
6. ______ Did I use correct subject-verb agreement?
7. ______ Did I check my spelling?
8. ______ Does every sentence have a subject and a verb?
9. ______ Did I use correct singular-plural agreement?
10. ______ Did I use correct word order?
11. ______ Is each word in the correct form?
12. ______ Did I use the correct verb tense for each verb?
13. ______ Are all of my sentences complete?

Lesson Eight
Comparison and Contrast

Introduction

We make comparisons all the time. We compare our present life to our past life. We compare people that we know. When we go shopping, we compare products. In making a comparison, we see if people or things are alike or different.

FOCUS Connecting Words of Contrast

We have already studied many connecting words. In this lesson, we will learn four new ones. These four connecting words show the reader that things, people, or ideas are different or opposite.

however	**on the other hand**
in contrast	**but**

However, in contrast, and *on the other hand* begin a new sentence. They introduce an idea that is opposite to the idea of the sentence (or paragraph) before. Here are some examples.

1. I have a dog. *However,* I don't have a cat.
2. They now have a dog and a cat. *On the other hand,* they didn't have any pets two years ago.
3. I have a dog. *In contrast,* John has a cat.

Look at the sentences in number 1. What is the subject of the first sentence? ______________ What is the subject of the second sentence? ______________

Look at the sentences in number 2. What is the subject of the first sentence? ______________ What is the subject of the second sentence? ______________

We usually use **however** and **on the other hand** to connect contrasting sentences when these sentences have the *same* subject.

Now look at number 3. Are the subjects of the two sentences the same or are they different? ________________________

We usually use **in contrast** to connect contrasting sentences which have different subjects.

FOCUS Punctuation

There are two ways we can punctuate these words.

1. George likes to play baseball. However, he doesn't like to watch it on television.
   George likes to play baseball. On the other hand, he doesn't like to watch it on television.
   George likes to play baseball. In contrast, his brother likes to watch it on television.

2. George likes to play baseball; however, he doesn't like to watch it on television.
   George likes to play baseball; on the other hand, he doesn't like to watch it on television.
   George likes to play baseball; in contrast, his brother likes to watch it on television.

Exercise A: Combine each pair of sentences. Use **however** or **on the other hand** if the two subjects are the same. Use **in contrast** if the two subjects are different. Rewrite the sentences. Use the correct punctuation.

1. Gloria is my sister. She is quite different from me.

____

2. Gloria has blond hair. I have brown hair.

____

3. My sister doesn't like tennis. She likes racquetball.

____

4. I don't know how to play raquetball. I play tennis very well.

____

5. My sister likes disco music and rock and roll. I prefer jazz and classical music.

____

6. My sister doesn't like to read. I read several books every month.

____

But also introduces an idea that is opposite to the idea before. *But* does not begin a new sentence. It is connected to the previous sentence with a comma.

We can use *but* if the two subjects are different.

Peter is from Lebanon, **but** Berthold is from Germany.

We can also use *but* if the two subjects are the same.

Peter speaks French and Arabic, **but** he doesn't speak Italian.

Exercise B: Connect each pair of sentences with **but**. Rewrite the new sentence. Check your punctuation.

1. Amir is from Malaysia. His best friend is from China.

___

2. Amir is tall and thin. Chan is short and plump.

___

3. Amir speaks Malay and English. He doesn't speak Chinese.

___

4. Amir likes classical music. Chan likes rock music.

___

5. Amir likes listening to music. He doesn't like dancing.

___

Exercise C: Punctuate each sentence.

1. Jae Wan is from Korea but Sven is from Sweden.
2. Jae Wan has black hair but Sven is blond.
3. Jae Wan speaks Korean and English however he doesn't speak Swedish.
4. Jae Wan wants to be a businessman In contrast Sven hopes to be a doctor.

5. Jae Wan likes business on the other hand he doesn't like science at all.

FOCUS Some Useful Vocabulary for Making Comparisons

1. Can you use these words correctly?

different-difference **similar-similarity**

Look at the underlined word in each pair of sentences. Which is the noun? Which is the adjective?

A. There are some differences between Amir and Chan.
Their hobbies are different.

B. Their personalities are similar.
The similarities between them are more important than the differences.

Exercise D: Circle the correct word from each pair in parentheses.

George and Anita are (different/difference) in many ways. These (differences/different) will become clearer. For example, they have (different/difference) hobbies. The biggest (difference/different) is that their personalities are so (different/difference). You can see that they are not at all (similar/similarity). It will surprise you to learn that they have (similar/similarity) friends.

2. Using **both**

Both means two people or two things. We use the word *both* to show that two things or two people are alike.

Example: Japan and Indonesia are two interesting countries. *Both* of them are in Asia, but there are some differences between them.

Exercise E: Combine each pair of sentences using **both . . . and.** Then change the sentence so that you use the correct pronoun.

Example: John likes to play tennis. Mark likes to play tennis.
Both John and Mark like to play tennis.
Both of them like to play tennis.

1. Saudi Arabians speak Arabic. Syrians speak Arabic.

____

____

2. Arabic is an interesting language. Chinese is an interesting language.

____

____

3. Nancy wants to learn Arabic. I want to learn Arabic.

____

____

4. You are studying English. I am studying English.

____

____

FOCUS Using the Writing Process

Step 1: Generating Ideas

One interesting topic for a composition is a comparison between two countries. Of course, it is not possible to compare every aspect of two countries in one composition. It is better to focus on one area.

Now make a list of some possible topics to focus on. You can write the topics here. Here are two suggestions to help you get started.

clothing
music

____

____

____

____

____

In the following composition, Shilpa, a student from India, compared Japan and Indonesia. She decided to compare some of the customs and courtesies of each country.

First, she wrote down the main areas she wanted to write about.

greetings and common courtesies
dating and marriage

Then she found some information for each area. She interviewed some students from these countries, and she did some reading in the library.

Step 2: Organizing Ideas

Shilpa organized her information into *categories* (groups). In this way, she could easily see how Japan and Indonesia were alike and how they were different.

	Japan	*Indonesia*
Greetings/ Courtesies	*Bow from the waist* *Don't shake hands*	*Shake hands* *Bow head slightly*
	Remove shoes before entering a house	*Same*

	Japan	Indonesia
Dating/ Marriage	A recent phenomenon Used to be arranged	Same
	Couples today make own choice, but consult with family	Marriage of choice very common in urban areas.
		A man can have up to four wives (Islamic law)

Step 3: Writing the First Draft

As you recall from Lessons 3 and 5, your introduction has an important purpose. It tells the reader what your topic is. It should give some general information about your topic without being *too* general. It should focus on your topic, and it should be interesting.

Exercise F: Read the following introductions. Choose the introduction you think is best for Shilpa's composition. Explain why you chose it.

1. Japan and Indonesia are two interesting countries. Both of them are in Asia, but there are some differences between them.
2. If you compare any countries, you will always find some differences. For example, Japan and Indonesia are two countries which are very different.
3. In this composition, I am going to show how Japan and Indonesia are different.

____

____

____

Step 4: Revising

A common mistake that students make is including information in a paragraph that does not belong because it does not fit the topic of that paragraph.

Exercise G: For each group of sentences, decide what the topic is. Then explain which sentence does not belong.

Group 1

a. Next are drinking customs.
b. People in Venezuela often drink thick, black coffee called *cafecito*.
c. In contrast, people in Indonesia drink boiled water.
d. People in both countries drink hot drinks.
e. The climate of both countries is hot.

1. Topic: ____

2. Sentence that does not belong: ____________________

3. Why? ____

____

4. What was the writer thinking of? ________________

____

5. Why did the writer include this sentence? __________

____

Group 2

a. Kuwait has a constitutional monarchy.
b. There are three branches of government: executive, legislative, and judicial.
c. The amir is the head of state.
d. The flag has three horizontal stripes: green, red, and white.
e. Men over the age of twenty-one can vote.

1. Topic: ______________________________

2. Sentence that does not belong: ______________________________

3. Why? ______________________________

____

4. What was the writer thinking of? ______________________________

____

5. Why did the writer include this sentence? ______________________________

____

Step 5: Rewriting

Here is the final draft of Shilpa's composition. Read it carefully.

Japan and Indonesia are two interesting countries. Both of them are in Asia, but there are some differences between them.

For example, Japanese greetings are different from Indonesian greetings. A bow from the waist is the traditional greeting in Japan. In contrast, Indonesians greet each other by shaking hands and bowing the head slightly. On the other hand, the customs for entering a house are similar. In both countries, people remove their shoes before entering a house.

In both countries, dating is something new. Traditionally, families arranged the marriages of young people. Today, in Japan young people usually choose their own husband or wife, but they usually consult with their families. In Indonesia, marriages of individual choice are very common, especially in urban areas. However, there is one big difference between the *two countries. As in other Muslim countries, an Indonesian man can have up to four wives.*

In summary, it is interesting to compare two countries located in the same part of the world and see some differences between them.

Things to Look at and Discuss

1. The first paragraph of a composition usually is the introduction. It gives the reader a general idea of what the composition is about. The other paragraphs provide *support* for this.
2. Reread Shilpa's introduction page 102. Her general topic is *Japan and Indonesia.* Her focus is *some differences between Japan and Indonesia.*
3. This *focus* has a special name. It is called the *thesis.* The thesis is the main idea of your composition. The purpose of the rest of your composition is to support your thesis. In other words, the rest of the paragraphs should show that your thesis is correct.
4. Each paragraph following the introduction supports the thesis with specific examples. Think of the thesis as a table top and the other paragraphs as the table legs. The legs are necessary to support the table top.
5. Shilpa's thesis is that there are some differences between Japan and Indonesia. The examples that she used for support include greetings, customs for entering a house, dating, and marriage.

Notice that the thesis is general, but the support is specific.

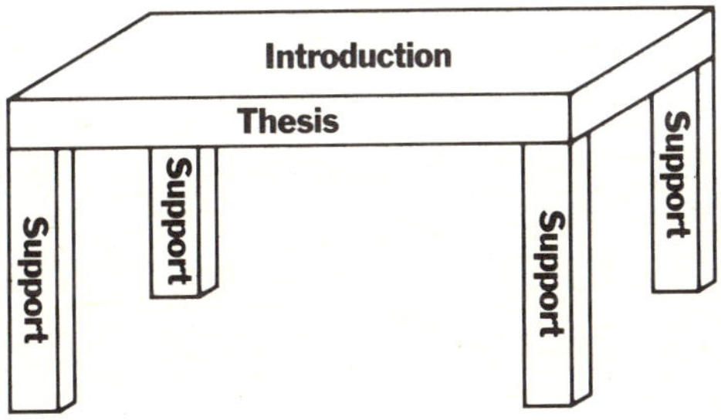

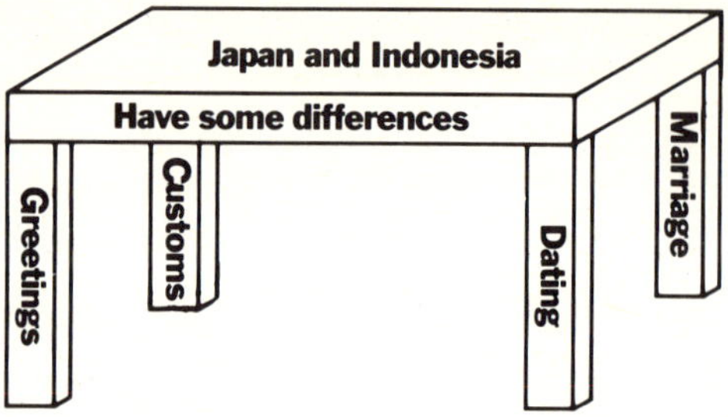

Exercise H: Work with two or three classmates. For each thesis below, write some examples that you could use for support.

Example: Thesis: My life in America is different in many ways from my life in my country.

I don't live with my family here in America.

I eat a lot of American food.

I don't know many people.

1. Thesis: My best friend and I are very much alike.

____

____

____

2. Thesis: There are a number of differences between married life and single life.

____

____

____

3. Thesis: Men and women in my country have very different roles.

Step 6: Conclusions

Reread Shilpa's last paragraph on page 103. What job does it do?

The last paragraph of this composition is a **conclusion.** A conclusion is a summary of your composition. It is similar to the introduction in several ways.

1. It is general.
2. It focuses on the thesis of the composition.

The simplest kind of conclusion is a restatement of the introduction. In other words, it states the same general idea as the introduction, but it uses different words. Some common connecting words used to write conclusions are **in summary, in conclusion,** and **to sum up.**

FOCUS Proofreading

By now, you should be very good at finding spelling, punctuation, and grammar mistakes.

Exercise I: These sentences have many kinds of mistakes. Work with a classmate and rewrite each sentence correctly.

1. There are many countries in the world but I am interested in two of them.

2. Japanese people generally bow several time to each other upon meeting.

3. The area is approximately 10,350 square mile.

4. In conclusion, this contries have different customs, religion, and government.
5. These countries has the same official language.
6. The United states has four season. But Malaysia only two.
7. The food in my country different from the food in venezuela.

Step 6: Choosing a Title

Did you notice that Shilpa's composition on page 102 does not have a title? Work with several classmates. Write several possible titles for the composition. Then compare your suggestions with those in your group.

Writing Assignment

Interview two people. They may be two classmates, teachers, friends, or neighbors. Use the information that you get from the interviews to write a composition comparing the two people.

What are some questions that you can ask in the interview? Work on the questions with your classmates. Write them down here.

___

___

___

___

___

___

___

____

____

____

Additional Topics for Writing

1. Compare your life in the United States with your life in your country.
2. Compare married life with single life.
3. Compare the role of men with the role of women in your country.
4. Compare your best friend with yourself.
5. Compare some aspect of your culture with that of another culture.

Follow these steps:

1. Talk about your topic with a classmate.
2. Write down your ideas. Connect related ideas.
3. Check the spelling of the words in your list of ideas.
4. Write your first draft.
5. Revise your first draft. Does your composition have a clear thesis? Does each additional paragraph support the thesis?
6. Rewrite. Remember that you can add or take away any information you want.
7. Write a short conclusion. Use one of the connecting words on page 105.
8. Proofread. Use the proofreading checklist below.
9. Choose a title.

Proofreading Checklist

Proofread for each type of mistake, one by one. When you finish proofreading for each point on the list, put a check mark (✔) in the space.

1. ______ Did I give my composition a title?

2. ______ Did I write the title with capital letters?
3. ______ Did I indent every new paragraph?
4. ______ Did I begin each sentence with a capital letter?
5. ______ Did I put a period at the end of every sentence?
6. ______ Did I use correct subject-verb agreement?
7. ______ Did I check my spelling?
8. ______ Does every sentence have a subject and a verb?
9. ______ Did I use correct singular-plural agreement?
10. ______ Did I use correct word order?
11. ______ Is each word in the correct form?
12. ______ Did I use the correct verb tense for each verb?
13. ______ Are all of my sentences complete?

Lesson Nine

Using Reasons and Examples for Support

Introduction

When you write a composition that explains your opinion, it is not enough simply to say what your opinion is. You must support your opinion with reasons, examples, or facts. Without support, your composition will be too general. You need to give specific reasons and examples to help the reader understand your opinion better.

FOCUS Connectors Used to Introduce Reasons and Examples

First, . . .	introduces your first reason
Second, . . .	introduces your second reason
Finally, . . .	introduces your last reason
For example, . . .	introduces an example
In addition, . . .	gives another example for the *same* idea
In other words, . . .	repeats the same idea, but uses different words. You can emphasize your ideas and make them clearer.

Note that all of the above connectors are followed by a comma.

Exercise A: Using Connecting Words. Fill in the spaces with a connecting word from the list below.

first	**for example**
second	**in addition**
finally	**in other words**

Why I Like Living in Colorado

Now that I have been living in Colorado for almost four years, I can say that I like it very much. ____________________, Colorado is a very beautiful state; the mountains are magnificent. ____________________, during the summer, they are covered with wildflowers. In the winter, they look beautiful covered with snow.

____________________, Colorado is a wonderful place for outdoor sports. ____________________, in the summer, you can go fishing or hiking. ____________________, it is fun to have a picnic in one of the parks. In the winter, you can go downhill or cross-country skiing. ____________________, it is easy to find something enjoyable to do.

____________________, Colorado has a very pleasant climate. It is never humid. The sun shines three hundred days a year. I think that I am lucky to live here!

FOCUS Using the Writing Process

Let's look at the steps Joel Castillo, a student from Venezuela, took when he wrote his composition.

Topic: why I prefer living in the city to living in the country.

Step 1: Generating Ideas

First, Joel wrote down his general reasons.

I prefer living in the city

more comfortable
more convenient
modern
work in an office
more interesting
more exciting

Step 2: Organizing Ideas

Joel grouped the ideas that seemed to belong together.

more comfortable
convenient
modern

more interesting
exciting

Then he wrote some specific examples for his ideas.
Here is the final draft of the composition.

A Better Life

I like living in the city better than living in the country for several reasons. First, city life is more modern and more comfortable than life in the country. For example, in the city, people live in a modern house or apartment. In addition, transportation is easy in the city. There are buses, trains, taxis, and subways.

Second, life in the city is more exciting than in the country. There is a lot of entertainment: movies, theaters, discos, clubs, restaurants, and many parties. In other words, there is a good night life.

Finally, I think that the city is more interesting than the country because there are many different kinds of people in the city. We can learn a lot from these people.

I enjoy the country for a vacation, but I prefer to live in the city.

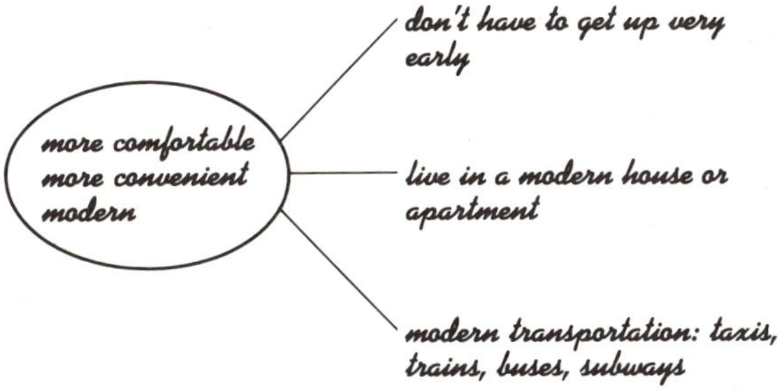

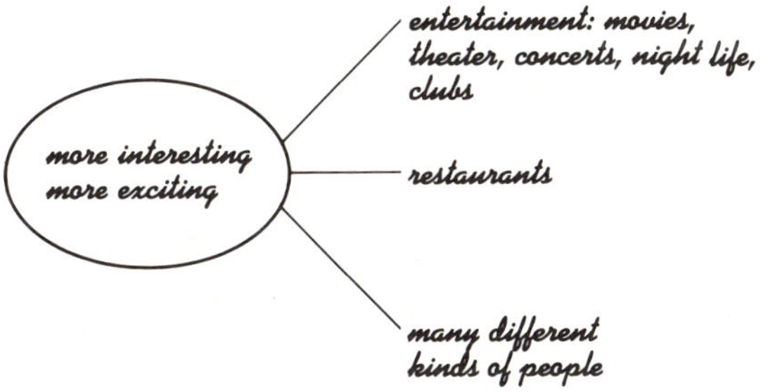

Things to Look at and Discuss

1. Compare the diagram above with the final draft on pages 112–113.
2. What is the job of the first sentence of the composition? Does it give you the main idea of the first paragraph, or does it give you the main idea of the whole composition?

3. What is the focus (main idea) of the first paragraph? What are the specific examples for this topic?

   Main idea: ______________________________

   Examples: 1. ______________________________

   2. ______________________________

4. What connecting word introduces the main idea of the first paragraph? Write the connecting word here: ____________
5. What connecting word introduces the *first example* for that main idea? Write that word here: ____________
6. What connecting word introduces the *second example* of that main idea? Write that word here: ____________
7. Look at paragraphs 1, 2, and 3. Find the three reasons that the writer gives for preferring to live in the city. What are they?

   Reasons: 1. ______________________________

   2. ______________________________

   3. ______________________________

   What is the connecting word used to introduce each reason?

   Connecting words: 1. ______________________________

   2. ______________________________

   3. ______________________________

8. In the second paragraph, find the connecting expression **in other words.** What does **in other words** mean? What job do you think it does in the paragraph?

____

Step 3: Writing the First Draft

FOCUS Using Reasons and Examples to Support Your Opinion

In a composition, you must support your opinion. You must give reasons for your opinion and support these reasons with specific examples.

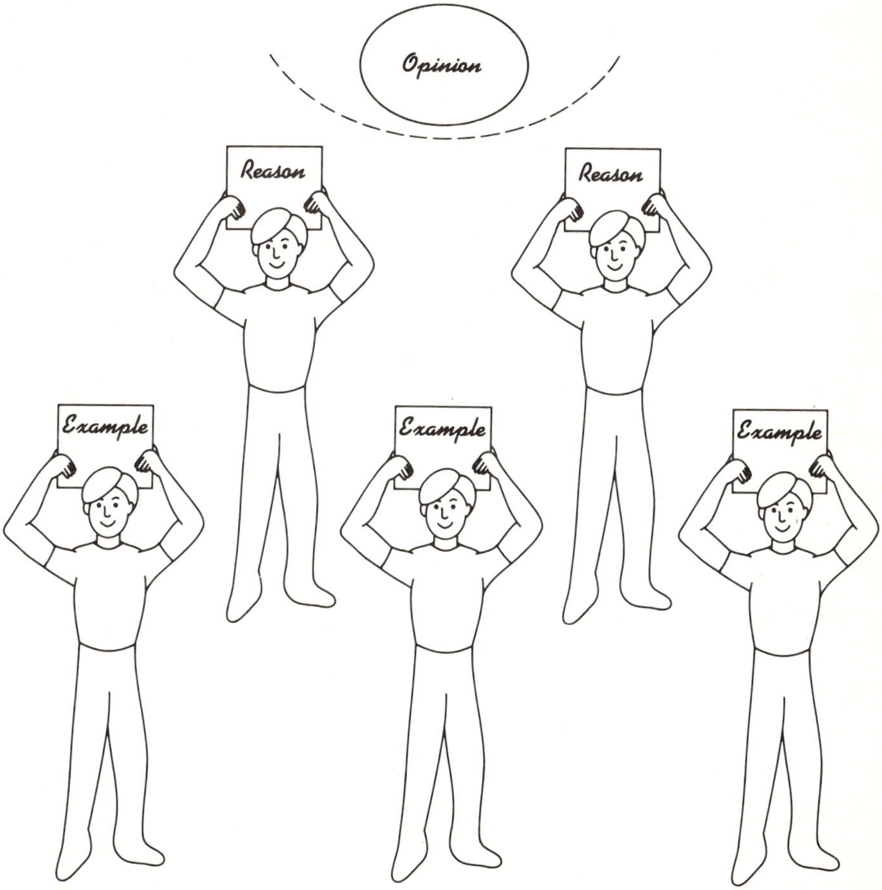

Let's look at an example of how this works.

Opinion: People shouldn't smoke.

Reasons
1. It is bad for your health.
2. It is a dirty habit.
3. It is expensive and a waste of money.

Exercise B: Here are some examples that support the reasons above. Match each example with the reason which it supports. Write the number of the reason (1, 2, or 3) in the space next to the example which supports it. The first one is done for you.

Examples

_1_ a. Smoking causes heart disease.

____ b. Smoking gives you bad breath.

____ c. One pack of cigarettes costs one dollar.

____ d. Ashtrays are dirty and smelly.

____ e. For the price of a week's worth of cigarettes, you can buy some good food.

____ f. Smoking causes lung cancer.

____ g. You could save almost thirty dollars a month by not smoking.

____ h. Smoke irritates your eyes.

____ i. Cigarettes turn your teeth yellow.

____ j. Cigarettes make your hands smell.

____ k. Smokers are more likely to get sick.

Exercise C: Write your own examples to support each reason.

Opinion: English is a valuable language to know.

Reason 1: It is useful for work.

Example: ____

____

____

Reason 2: It is useful for traveling.

Example: ____

____

____

Reason 3: It is useful for studying.

Example: ____

____

____

Exercise D: Work with a group of students. Write reasons and examples for the two opinions below.

> Note: You don't have to agree with an opinion to be able to support it!

Opinion 1: It is a good idea to get married when you are young.

Reason 1: ______________________________

____

____

Examples: ______________________________

____

____

Reason 2: ______________________________

____

____

Examples: ______________________________

____

____

Opinion 2: It is a good idea to get married when you are mature.

Reason 1: ______________________________

____

____

Examples: ______________________________

____

____

Reason 2: ______________________________

____

____

Examples: ______________________________

____

____

Step 4: Revision

FOCUS Using *because* Correctly

The word *because* is used to introduce reasons. It begins a clause that answers the question *Why?* The main clause of the sentence gives a result.

1. I am tired because I went to sleep late last night.

   (result: "I am tired"; reason: "I went to sleep late last night")

2. John studies hard because he wants to do well in class.

   (result: "John studies hard"; reason: "he wants to do well in class")

3. Mary was late because she had a flat tire.

   (result: "Mary was late"; reason: "she had a flat tire")

You can also begin the sentence with "Because + reason," but you must put a comma at the end of the reason clause.

1. Because I went to sleep late last night, I am tired.

   (reason: "I went to sleep late last night"; result: "I am tired")

2. Because you don't work hard, you don't get good grades.

   reason — result

3. Because I lost my book, I couldn't do the homework.

   reason — result

Sometimes it is easy to confuse the result with the reason when you are writing.

Exercise E: Decide which phrase is the result and which is the reason in each of the sentences below.

1. Mary studied for three hours because she wanted to get a high grade.

2. Mary was very nervous because she wanted to get a high grade.

3. Mary couldn't do this exercise because she didn't understand it.

4. Because Mary was late for the test, she couldn't finish it.

5. Mary was upset because she didn't finish the test.

6. Because she is a very good student, the teacher let her take the test again.

Exercise F: Decide if each sentence is correct and logical. In other words, does the word *because* introduce the *reason* in each sentence? If the sentence is not correct, rewrite it.

1. Lisa has lived in many different countries because she can speak many languages.

   ____

   ____

2. She speaks Spanish very well because she lived in Mexico for five years.

____

____

3. She can't understand French because she never studied it.

____

____

4. John is a good mechanic because he can fix many kinds of engines.

____

____

5. Because John is a good mechanic, many people bring him their cars.

____

____

6. John didn't fix my Fiat last night because he was sick.

____

____

7. I like living in the city because it is more exciting than living in the country.

8. Because I am happy living in New York, it is a big city.

9. The city has many discos and restaurants because it is more interesting than the country.

FOCUS Proofreading

1. Sentence fragments (frag)

In Lesson 7, you learned about sentence fragments. Remember, a sentence fragment is an incomplete sentence. For example,

Because I want to lose weight.

is not a complete sentence. To have a complete sentence, you must have both the reason and the result clauses. For example,

Because I want to lose weight, I will start a diet tomorrow.

or

I will start a diet tomorrow because I want to lose weight.

are complete sentences.

Exercise G: In each paragraph, correct the sentence fragment.

1. I really enjoy traveling. Each year I try to take an interesting trip to a new place. However, I can't take a trip this year. I don't have enough money. Because I bought a new car.

2. There are many reasons why I like traveling. First, I enjoy seeing new places and meeting new people. In addition, because every place has different kinds of food. I learn to eat many new things.

2. Run-on sentences (rs)

You can think of a run-on sentence as the opposite of a sentence fragment. You make a run-on sentence when you put two complete sentences together. A run-on sentence should be two separate sentences. Here is an example.

Last year I went to Italy and I went to Rome and Florence.

The above sentence should be

Last year I went to Italy. I went to Rome and Florence.

Exercise H: Correct the run-on sentences.

1. In Rome, I visited Vatican City and I saw Saint Peter's Church and the Vatican Museum and then I visited the Roman Forum.
2. Saint Peter's is a very beautiful church and it has a lot of famous paintings and sculptures.
3. I think Florence is my favorite city. It has many beautiful works of art and it is quieter than Rome and smaller, too.

4. I did a lot of shopping in Florence and I bought some beautiful shoes and I also bought a leather jacket.

3. Comma splice (cs)

A common mistake that many students make is to connect two complete sentences with a comma. You *cannot* connect two complete sentences with a comma. You must use a period. For example,

I especially enjoyed the food in Italy, I ate many kinds of salad and pasta.

The above sentence should be

I especially enjoyed the food in Italy. I ate many kinds of salad and pasta.

Exercise I: Correct the comma splices in this paragraph.

One of the most beautiful sculptures in Florence, Italy is Michelangelo's *David,* the sculpture is very tall and stands in the middle of a large room. The lighting is natural, it comes through the windows in the ceiling. The statue is about five and a half meters tall, it is made of pure white marble.

Exercise J: General Proofreading Let's see what you remember from the other lessons in this book. The paragraph below has several different kinds of mistakes. Read the paragraph carefully to find them. Rewrite the paragraph. Then compare your rewrite with a classmate's.

Because Switzerland is a little country. We have only a few traditions. There is a tradition very important, august first, the National Day, on this day people light many fire to say to the world, "On this day switzerland was born."

Step 5: Choosing a Title

By now, you should be able to choose an interesting title for your composition. When you choose a title, you must think about your topic. You also want to catch the reader's eye with something interesting. Let's look at this topic for an example.

Topic: Why I decided to get married

One possible title for this topic might be "A Major Decision." Can you think of some other good titles? Work with a classmate.

Writing Assignment

Choose one of these topics for a composition.

1. Why it is important to learn English.
2. Why you decided to get (or not get) married.
3. Explain your reasons for studying English in this school.
4. Explain why children should not (or should) watch television.
5. Why it is important to have friends.
6. Why living in a foreign country is a valuable experience.

Follow these steps.

1. Write down your reasons.
2. Write some examples for each reason.
3. Discuss your reasons and examples with a classmate.
4. Write your first draft.
5. Revise.

6. Write your second draft.
7. Proofread. Use the proofreading checklist below.
8. Choose a title.

Proofreading Checklist

Proofread for each type of mistake, one by one. When you finish proofreading for each point on the list, put a check mark (✔) in the space.

1. ______ Did I give my composition a title?
2. ______ Did I write the title with capital letters?
3. ______ Did I indent every new paragraph?
4. ______ Did I begin each sentence with a capital letter?
5. ______ Did I put a period at the end of every sentence?
6. ______ Did I use correct subject-verb agreement?
7. ______ Did I check my spelling?
8. ______ Does every sentence have a subject and a verb?
9. ______ Did I use correct singular-plural agreement?
10. ______ Did I use the correct word order?
11. ______ Is each word in the correct form?
12. ______ Did I use the correct verb tense for each verb?
13. ______ Are all of my sentences complete?
14. ______ Are there any other sentence errors (run-ons, comma splices)?

Appendix

Proofreading Symbols
Capitalization Rules
Punctuation Rules
Glossary

Proofreading Symbols

Proofreading marks are listed in the order in which they are presented in the textbook.

cap	You need a capital letter.
p	You have a mistake in punctuation.
sp	You have a spelling mistake.
¶	You need a new paragraph. Indent.
agr	You have a mistake in agreement.
wo	Wrong word order.
^	You forgot a word.
wf	Wrong form of a word.
tns	Wrong verb tense.
frag	You have an incomplete sentence.
rs	Run-on sentence.
cs	Comma splice.

Capitalization Rules

Beginnings of Sentences
The first word in a sentence is capitalized.

Someone is knocking at the door.

Words in a Title
The first word, the last word, and all other important words in a title are capitalized. Unless they are the first or last word in the title, the words *a, an,* and *the* and connectors are usually not capitalized.

The Last of the Mohicans
Romeo and Juliet

Names of People
Capitalize all names of people.

John Blake Whitney   F. G. Harkness
Chang Tsin Hai   Emily

Names of Places
Capitalize the names of specific places.

Europe, Lake Erie, Kentucky, Central Park, Boston
Pine Street, Cleveland Museum of Art, Mount Vesuvius

Names of Schools, Companies, Buildings
Capitalize the names of schools, companies, and buildings.

University of Southern California
International Business Machines
World Trade Center

Days of the Week
Capitalize days of the week.

Tuesday, Wednesday, Friday, Sunday

Months of the Year
Capitalize months of the year.

March, April, October, November

Languages and Nationalities
Capitalize the names of languages and nationalities.

Swedish, Malaysian, Peruvian, Canadian, Swahili

Famous Places and Landmarks
Capitalize the names of famous places and landmarks.

the Grand Canyon, the George Washington Bridge

The Word *I*
Always capitalize the word *I*.

After school, I will go home.

Punctuation Rules

The Period
Use a period at the end of a sentence that is not an exclamation or a question.

We learned to speak French last year.
Go to the corner and turn right.

The Comma
Use a comma between the name of a city and a country.

She was born in Rio de Janiero, Brazil.

Use a comma between the name of a city and a state.

New Orleans, Louisiana

Use a comma between the date and the year.

December 5, 1985

Use a comma between the day and the month.

Monday, October 31

Use a comma between two or more adjectives that precede a noun if the adjectives are not quantifiers (*some, several, many, a few*).

The library is a cool, quiet place to study.
Many successful people speak several different languages.
The tall, handsome man sat down to read the newspaper.

Use a comma after connectors such as *furthermore, in addition, moreover, however, in contrast,* and *on the other hand.*

I studied the history of the countries I planned to visit. *In addition,* I learned to speak the languages spoken there.
He enjoys playing chess; *furthermore,* he plays it very well.
She plays the piano very well; *in contrast,* she cannot sing on key.

Use a comma after an introductory phrase or clause.

After reading his paper, I understood his feelings about his childhood much better.
Although I have been studying for several hours, I am still nervous about the test.
If you write her a letter, she will answer it.
I understood his feelings about his childhood much better after reading his paper.
I am still nervous about the test although I have been studying for several hours.
She will answer your letter if you write to her.

Use a comma to set off an idea that is opposite to the idea before.

Alice speaks Spanish, but she does not speak German.
Henry's sister, not his brother, is a teacher.

Use a comma to separate items in a series.

Francesca bakes delicious bread, muffins, and rolls.
I brought the following supplies: pencils, pens, paper, and a ruler.

The Colon

Use a colon before a list of items following an independent clause.

I ordered the complete dinner: vegetable soup, steak, salad, and apple pie.

The Semicolon
Use a semicolon to connect two sentences that are closely related.

Bill fished every morning for a week; he only caught five fish all week.
Angela plays basketball; however, she has never played soccer.
The students held a car wash to raise money for the trip; in addition, they raised money by selling cookies.

The Question Mark
Use a question mark at the end of a question.

Did the bus arrive on time?

The Apostrophe
Use an apostrophe to indicate letters left out in a contraction.

She didn't finish reading the assignment.

Quotation Marks
Enclose a direct quotation in quotation marks.

"I have already walked and fed the dog," Lorenzo said.

The Exclamation Point
Use the exclamation point to end an exclamation.

Look at that beautiful sunrise!

The Hyphen
Use a hypen when you come to the end of a line and it is necessary to divide a word.

Ernesto and his wife, Luisa, waved happily as they got off the bus.

Glossary

ADJECTIVE One of the parts of speech. An adjective is a word or phrase that modifies (changes, describes, or limits the meaning of) a noun or pronoun.

> The *blue* sky began to fill with *white, puffy* clouds.
> *Her older* cousin is *tall* and *thin*.
> *Exhausted*, he collapsed on *that* bench.

ADVERB One of the parts of speech. An adverb is a word or phrase that modifies (changes, describes, or limits the meaning of) a verb, an adjective, or another adverb.

> Rain fell *heavily*.
> The *very* wet puppy cried.
> I raise my hand *more often* now.

CATEGORY A group.

> Plants such as spinach, lettuce, and swiss chard are in the category of green, leafy vegetables.

CAUSE AND RESULT A type of reasoning that helps establish order among ideas by giving the reason (cause) of an effect and then giving the effect (result).

> If you understand the directions, you will be able to follow them.

CHRONOLOGICAL ORDER Events listed in the order in which they happened, starting with the first and concluding with the last.

> She described her day chronologically from the moment she woke up until she crawled back into bed at night.

CIRCLE DIAGRAM A chart in the shape of a circle that helps to organize ideas.

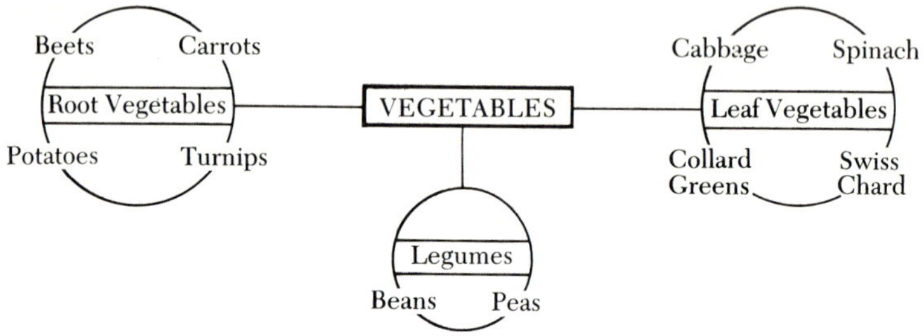

COMBINING SENTENCES Putting two or more sentences together into one by using various connecting words and punctuation marks.

> The train was late. It was very crowded.
> The train was late and very crowded.

> Ann ordered lasagna. Carl ordered lasagna.
> Both Ann and Carl ordered lasagna.

> I have a cousin who lives in Italy. I have an aunt who lives in England. I have several relatives who live in Greece.

> I have a cousin who lives in Italy and an aunt who lives in England; in addition, I have several relatives who live in Greece.

> Bill enjoys playing soccer. He does not enjoy playing tennis.
> Bill enjoys playing soccer but not tennis.

COMMA SPLICE The incorrect joining of two sentences into a run-on sentence with only a comma separating them. To correct a comma splice, the sentences should be separated into two sentences, or a connector should be added after the comma, or a semicolon should be used instead of the comma.

> The plane was delayed because of bad weather, the people waiting for it to land grew impatient.

COMPARISON AND CONTRAST An organization of ideas according to similarities and differences.

Both Elena and Rodrigo speak French well, but only Rodrigo speaks German.

COMPLEMENT A word or group of words that comes after the verb in a sentence and that adds information to the verb.

They gave *her a surprise party.*
He was a *member of the club.*

COMPOUND SUBJECT Two or more subjects in one simple sentence.

Federico and *Gretchen* are exchange students.

COMPOUND VERB Two or more verbs in one simple sentence.

Frank *went* to the store, *picked* up the groceries, *came* home, and *prepared* us a delicious dinner.

CONCLUSION A summary of a composition that often restates the general idea of the introduction in different words.

Finally, let me remind you that the privileges of citizenship are accompanied by responsibilities.

CONDITIONAL Something dependent on something else.

If you want to go with us, you should ready.

CONNECTORS Words that show the relationship between words, phrases, or sentences.

Karen is studying Italian *and* French. *Furthermore,* she wants to travel to Italy *and* France next year.
First, you must turn on the power. *Then,* you can insert the disc in the computer.
If you know how to play the piano, you can teach me.
You will be able to play the piano better *if* you practice.
She speaks well; *however,* she writes even better.
Arnold likes dogs, *but* Sam prefers cats.

DESCRIPTION (PHYSICAL) Explanation that enables the reader to picture what the thing being discussed is like.

Amanda was one meter and sixty-eight centimeters tall, weighed fifty kilos, had brown hair and blue eyes, and was considered to be attractive by all who knew her.

DESCRIPTION (PERSONALITY) Explanation of traits other than physical.

His thoughtfulness endeared him to his friends.

DIAGRAM A drawing, sketch, plan, or chart that makes something easier to understand.

Diagram of a Friendly Letter

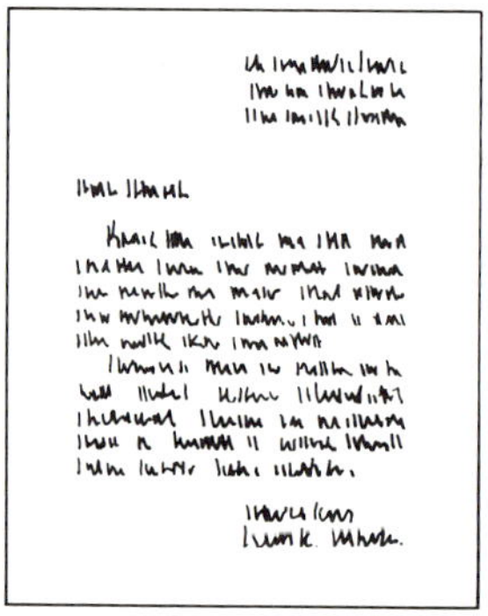

EXAMPLE A representative sample or model.

Japan is an example of an industrialized Asian country.

FACT Something that actually exists or occurs.

He was born on February 6, 1954.

FIRST DRAFT A preliminary piece of writing that will be revised and corrected in following stages.

FOCUS A central or specific point.

In my paper about art, I plan to focus on the work of the Impressionists.

FRAGMENT Part of sentence that is incorrectly punctuated as a sentence.

The travelers waiting in line at the airport.
Flying through the cloudless sky at thirty thousand feet.
At the library.

GENERAL IDEAS Broad ideas that are not specific or focused.

An example of a general idea is *politics.*

GENERAL TOPIC A broad topic that is not specific or focused.

An example of a general topic might be *animals.*

GENERATING IDEAS Producing ideas (often used when focusing a topic or gathering support for a topic).

GROUP A number of individuals or items related by a common factor.

Oranges, lemons, limes, and grapefruit belong to the food group called citrus fruits.

INTRODUCTION The opening remarks and background information that present the focus or main point and the purpose of a piece of writing.

LIST a series of items (often created when generating ideas).

INDONESIA
geography
history
crops
people
industry

LOGICAL ORDER Any arrangement that is easy to follow and easy to understand. Types of logical orders include chronological (or time sequence) order, spatial order, cause and result, inductive approach (stating pieces of evidence and then a conclusion), deductive approach (stating a general principle and then giving examples of it), and order of importance.

NARRATION A story told in chronological order.

NOUN One of the parts of speech. A noun is a word that names a person, place, or thing.

> *Derek, Girl, house, New Delhi, horse, basket,* and *love* are all nouns.

OPINION A belief or judgment.

> I think she would make a good president.

ORGANIZATION OF IDEAS Arranging related ideas in groups under the same topic or in some logical order.

PARAGRAPH A group of sentences about the same idea or topic.

PROCESS A series of steps necessary to reach a certain result or goal.

> The process of bread baking involves mixing the ingredients together, allowing the dough to rise, kneading the dough, and baking the bread.

PROOFREADING Making corrections in spelling, grammar, usage, punctuation, and capitalization as the final step in the writing process.

REASONS Statements that explain an action or an opinion.

> His success in school was due to hard work and intelligence.

REVISING Changing a piece of writing to improve its organization, support, or wording. Revising is the step in the writing process that follows writing the first draft.

REWRITING The step in the writing process that follows revising and in which a second draft is written that incorporates the changes made during revising.

RUN-ON SENTENCE Two or more sentences that are punctuated incorrectly as though they were one.

The library was closed, we forgot it was a holiday.

SIMPLE SENTENCE One independent clause that has a subject and a verb and can stand by itself as a complete sentence. A simple sentence may also have a compound subject and/or a compound verb.

Stefan went to Poland.
Maria and Kathleen bought tickets to the concert but were unable to go.

SINGULAR-PLURAL AGREEMENT Making sure that singular subjects have singular verbs and that plural subjects have plural verbs.

One student was absent yesterday.
The three books that I read last week were all interesting.

SPECIFIC EXAMPLES Definite samples or models.

Spanish, Portuguese, Swahili, and Hindi are specific examples of languages.

SPECIFIC IDEAS Narrow, specific, focused ideas.

The general idea of literature can be narrowed to the specific idea of Shakespeare's historical plays.

SUPPORT Reasons, examples, and facts used to develop a piece of writing.

THESIS The main idea of a piece of writing.

TITLE The name given to a work.

The title of his paper was "How to Choose the Perfect Gift."

TREE DIAGRAM A chart that branches out from a general idea to more specific ones.

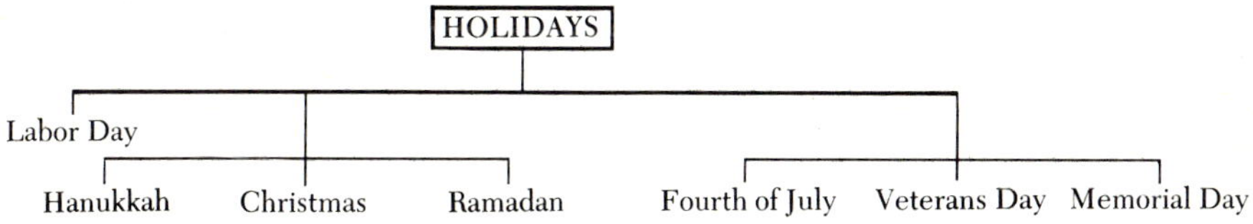

VERB TENSE A form of a verb that shows time of action. A verb is one of the parts of speech. A verb is a word or group of words that shows an action, a condition, or the fact that something exists.

> I sing. I sang. I will sing. I have sung. I had sung. I will have sung.

WRITING PROCESS The steps used in producing a piece of writing. The steps include generating ideas, organizing ideas, writing a first draft, revising, rewriting, proofreading, and choosing a title.

STUDENT QUESTIONNAIRE

In preparing the second edition of WRITE IT DOWN, we would appreciate your evaluation of the present edition. Your suggestions will definitely affect the contents of the second edition. Please return this questionnaire to the Education Editor, College Department, Holt, Rinehart and Winston, 383 Madison Avenue, New York, N.Y. 10017

Name ______________________ Date ______________________

School ______________________ Course title ______________________

Instructor ______________________

1. Did you find this book too easy? ________ too difficult? ________

   about right? ________
2. Which sections did you find most helpful? Which sections did you find least helpful?

Lesson One Basic Mechanics

	Helpful	*Not helpful*
Focus: Punctuation marks and their names	______	______
Focus: Rules for composition titles	______	______
Focus: How your composition should look	______	______
Focus: Basic capitalization and punctuation rules	______	______
Focus: Proofreading symbols	______	______
Sentence boundaries	______	______
Writing Assignment	______	______

Lesson Two The Writing Process

Focus: The writing process	______	______
Focus: General topics and specific examples	______	______
Focus: Using the writing process	______	______
Focus: Proofreading symbols	______	______
Writing assignment	______	______

Lesson Three Describing an Object

Focus: Choosing a general topic and focusing
Focus: Using the writing process
Focus: Logical order
Focus: Writing an introduction
Focus: Proofreading symbols
Writing assignment
Proofreading checklist

Lesson Four Describing a Place

Focus: Punctuation: Using the colon
Focus: Choosing a topic
Focus: Using the writing process
Focus: Combining sentences with the same topic
Focus: Combining sentences by putting adjectives before the noun
Focus: Combining sentences using *and*
Focus: Making sure your sentences are correct
Focus: Proofreading symbols
Writing assignment
Proofreading checklist

Lesson Five Describing a Person

Focus: Connecting words to add information
Focus: Punctuation
Focus: Using the writing process
Focus: Proofreading symbols
Focus: Adverbs
Writing assignment
Proofreading checklist

Lesson Six Narration

Focus: Connecting words—chronological order
Focus: Using the writing process
Focus: More practice writing introductions
Focus: Proofreading symbols
Writing assignment
Proofreading checklist

Lesson Seven Process

Focus: More practice with chronological order	______	______
Focus: Punctuation	______	______
Focus: Using the writing process	______	______
Focus: Punctuation	______	______
Focus: Proofreading symbols	______	______
Writing assignment	______	______
Proofreading checklist	______	______

Lesson Eight Comparison and Contrast

Focus: Connecting words of contrast	______	______
Focus: Punctuation	______	______
Focus: Some useful vocabulary for making comparisons	______	______
Focus: Using the writing process	______	______
Focus: Proofreading	______	______
Writing assignment	______	______
Additional Topics for writing	______	______
Proofreading checklist	______	______

Lesson Nine Using Reasons and Examples for Support

Focus: Connecting words—introduce reasons and examples	______	______
Focus: Using the writing process	______	______
Focus: Using reasons and examples to support your opinion	______	______
Focus: Using *because* correctly	______	______
Focus: Proofreading	______	______
Writing assignment	______	______
Proofreading checklist	______	______

Appendix

Proofreading Symbols	______	______
Capitalization Rules	______	______
Punctuation Rules	______	______
Glossary	______	______